Saxon **MATH**

Course 2

Stephen Hake

Instructional Masters

SAXON™

A Harcourt Achieve Imprint

www.SaxonPublishers.com

1-800-284-7019

ISBN 1-5914-1869-0

1 2 3 4 5 6 7 8 202 14 13 12 11 10 09 08 07

Instructional Masters

Saxon Math Course 2 Instructional Masters contains a Performance Task Scoring Guide with Rubrics, a Parent Letter, Lesson Recording Forms, daily Power-Up activities, a Student Progress Chart, Performance Tasks and Activities, and Lesson and Investigation Activity Masters. Brief descriptions of these components are provided below.

Performance Task Scoring Guide with Rubrics

This book contains a Performance Task Scoring Guide with teacher and student rubrics to assist you with the evaluation and scoring of student performance on both Performance Tasks and Performance Activities.

Parent Letter

Parental involvement greatly improves a student's chance for success. When parents understand what is being asked of their children in school, they can provide support at home. The parent letter explains the keys to success in the Saxon mathematics program. An English and a Spanish version are provided. At the beginning of the year, give each student one copy to take to his or her parents. To ensure that the parents receive the letters, you might require the students to return the letters bearing their parents' signatures. Alternatively, you could mail the letters directly to the parents.

Recording Forms

This book contains two kinds of recording forms you might find useful. The Lesson Recording Forms are designed to help you track and analyze student performance on lessons. The Student Progress Chart is designed to help students track and analyze their daily Facts practice performance.

Answer Form A: Lesson Worksheet

This is a single-page master with check boxes for daily activities, answer blanks for Power-Up activities, and partitions for recording the solutions to twelve Practice Set problems.

Answer Form B: Written Practice Solutions

This is a double-page master with a grid background and partitions for recording the solutions to 30 problems.

Answer Form C: Written Practice Solutions

This is a double-page master with a plain, white background and partitions for recording the solutions to 30 problems.

Form D: Student Progress Chart

This is a single-page master with boxes for recording the time and score of each Power-Up Facts practice. Give one to each student so he or she can monitor Facts practice performance throughout the year.

Power Up

Each instructional day begins with a Power-Up activity which should be administered before every lesson. The Power Up is an integral part of the daily program. Each Power Up contains a set of math **Facts,** eight **Mental Math** problems, and a **Problem Solving** activity. Students benefit from the daily practice of math facts, mental math, and problem-solving skills.

Facts

Students are expected to master a variety of mathematical facts, skills, and vocabulary. Daily Facts practice enhances the retention of this learning. Facts practice covers content that students should be able to recall immediately. Rapid and accurate recall of basic facts, skills, and vocabulary dramatically increases students' mathematical powers. Mastery of basic facts frees students to focus on procedures and concepts rather than computation. Employing memory to recall frequently encountered facts permits students to bring higher-level thinking skills to bear when solving problems.

Mental Math

The Mental Math problem set follow Facts practice. Students should perform calculations mentally without the aid of paper and pencil or the use of a calculator. Mental math ability pays lifelong benefits and improves markedly with practice.

Problem Solving

A Problem Solving activity follows Mental Math. Each problem provides students with the opportunity to develop and practice problem-solving strategies using a four-step problem-solving process to communicate mathematical ideas. With daily practice, students can become powerful problem solvers.

Administering Facts

Reproduce the Power Up indicated for each lesson and provide a copy to each student.* On the first presentation of a Facts practice set, you may choose to make the practice instructional by working through the problems with the students and providing the answers. However, students should work independently and rapidly during all subsequent practices of the same Facts sheet, racing to improve on previous performances.

* As an alternative to copying a Power Up for each student every day, provide each student with a *Saxon Math Course 2 Power-Up Workbook*, which contains all the Power Ups required for one student for one year.

Each Power Up contains a line for students to record their Facts practice times. Students should also record their time and score on a copy of the Student Progress Chart (Form D). Timing students is motivating. Striving to improve speed helps to automate skills and offers the additional benefit of an up-tempo atmosphere for the class. Time invested in Facts practice is repaid in the students' ability to work faster. Allow five minutes or less for Facts practice.

Quickly read answers at the conclusion of the Facts practice. (The answers are found in the *Solutions Manual* and at the bottom of the daily lesson page in the *Teacher's Manual*.) Students should correct errors and complete the sheet as part of the day's assignment if they are unable to finish within the allotted time.

Administering Mental Math and Problem Solving

At the conclusion of Facts practice, begin the Mental Math problem set. Allow two or three minutes to complete the Mental Math portion of each Power Up. Then review the correct answers with the class. Instruct students to correct any mistakes.

The problem-solving exercise should be approached as a whole-class activity, providing a rich problem-solving experience for all students. Encourage students to propose a problem-solving strategy. Then, as a group, apply the four-step problem-solving process to the problem. Instruct students to record the problem-solving strategy and the solution to the problem on their Power-Up sheet.

Most problem-solving exercises can be solved in a few minutes. The entire Power Up should take less than 15 minutes to complete.

Performance Task and Activity Masters

The Performance Tasks and Activities are exercises to be given after students complete a Cumulative Test. These activities are supported by Performance Task and Activity masters which should be copied from this book as directed in the *Teacher's Manual*. The Activities are concise assignments that are designed to be completed in class. The Tasks are extended real-world or cross-curricular projects.

Test day should be structured so that students complete a Power-Up Test, a Cumulative Test, and a Performance Task or Activity. The materials, suggested preparations, time requirements, and procedures for each Performance Task or Activity are described in the corresponding Cumulative Assessment section of the *Saxon Math Course 2 Teacher's Manual*.

Administering a Performance Task or Activity

After each Cumulative Test, distribute one copy of the suggested Performance Task or Activity master(s) to each student and conduct the activity using the instruction in the *Teacher's Manual*. Students who do not complete the Performance Task or Activity in class can complete it as homework. To provide maximum time for the Cumulative Test and Performance Task or Activity, we recommend that no homework be collected or reviewed on test day.

Assessing Performance Tasks and Activities

Every Performance Task and Activity can be assessed using the Performance Task Scoring Guide and the Rubrics provided in this book. To check students' work, refer to the Performance Task and Activity solutions section in the *Solutions Manual*.

Lesson and Investigation Activity Masters

Selected lessons and investigations in the student textbook present content through activities. Often these activities require the use of Lesson or Investigation Activity sheets. These Activity masters should be photocopied for students to use during the appropriate lesson or investigation. The *Teacher's Manual* indicates when to photocopy these masters and how many copies to make. Although the activity sheets support specific lessons and investigations, they can also be used throughout the school year to complement instruction and review.

We suggest that the fraction manipulatives (Investigation Activity masters 4–9) be photocopied on six different colors of paper or that students color-code their copies of the fraction manipulatives before cutting them. Some of these masters are worksheets. Answers to these worksheets can be found in the *Solutions Manual*.

Generic rubrics are a helpful evaluation tool for use with Performance Tasks and Activities which do not have a single correct answer. They are especially useful for evaluating a wide range of student responses to complex multi-step tasks that can be executed with multiple problem-solving strategies.

Teacher Rubric

Use the Teacher Rubric to evaluate student performance and score the Performance Tasks and Activities. The Rubric provides descriptors to ensure consistent, unbiased scoring. The four-point scale permits valid differentiation of the range and degree of quality of student work and allows for scoring on a continuum.

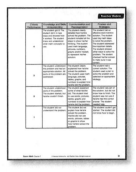

Student performance should be judged on the basis of three criteria:

1. **Knowledge and Skills Understanding:** Assesses the student's knowledge of mathematical concepts and the application of mathematical skills to solve the problems presented in a Performance Task or Activity.

2. **Communication and Representation:** Assesses the student's ability to communicate solutions to mathematical problems and to represent mathematical concepts with language, symbols, numbers, pictures, graphs, and models.

3. **Process and Strategies:** Assesses the student's problem-solving strategy and the plan and the process utilized to arrive at a solution.

You can use the Teacher Rubric to collectively judge overall performance based on the criteria listed above, or you can score each category independently and average the scores. Read and evaluate student performances and assign a score of 1–4.

Student Rubric

Distribute a copy of the Student Rubric to each student prior to administering Performance Task 1.

- Review the rubric with the class.

- Explain that a rubric is a set of scoring guidelines used to accurately and fairly evaluate student work.

- Describe the three categories used to evaluate student work.

- Describe the four possible scores and how the different levels of quality are distinguished from one another.

- Encourage students to use the rubric to evaluate and self-assess their own work before turning in a Performance Task or Activity.

- Instruct students to use the rubric to verify their score and self-correct their work when Performance Tasks and Activities are returned.

Criteria Performance	Knowledge and Skills Understanding	Communication and Representation	Process and Strategies
4	The student got it! The student did it in new ways and showed how it worked. The student knew and understood what math concepts to use.	The student clearly detailed how he/she solved the problem. The student included all the steps to show his/her thinking. The student used math language, pictures, numbers, graphs and/or models to represent his/her solution.	The student had an effective and inventive solution. The student used big math ideas to solve the problem. The student addressed the important details. The student showed other ways to solve the problem. The student checked his/her answer to make sure it was correct.
3	The student understood the problem and had an appropriate solution. All parts of the problem are addressed.	The student clearly explained how he/she solved the problem. The student used math language, pictures, tables, graphs, and numbers to explain how he/she did the problem.	The student had a correct solution. The student used a plan to solve the problem and selected an appropriate strategy.
2	The student understood parts of the problem. The student started, but he/she couldn't finish.	The student explained some of what he/she did. The student tried to use words, pictures, tables, graphs and numbers to explain how he/she did the problem.	The student had part of the solution, but did not know how to finish. The student was not sure if he/she had the correct answer. The student needed help.
1	The student did not understand the problem.	The student did not explain how he/she solved the problem. He/she did not use words, pictures, tables or graphs to show how he/she solved the problem.	The student couldn't get started. The student did not know how to begin.

Student Evaluation	Knowledge and Skills Understanding	Communication and Representation	Process and Strategies
4	I understand and can prove my understanding in more than one way.	I explained my work in detail and justified my answer. I showed my work in great detail and illustrated my thinking.	I selected the most appropriate strategy and used the process to solve the problem.
3	I understand the task and can show that I understand.	I can explain my thinking. I can show my work.	I selected a strategy and followed the process.
2	I have some understanding of the task.	I can explain some of my thinking. I can show some of my work.	I selected a strategy but became confused on the process.
1	I need help in understanding the task.	I need help in explaining my thinking. I need help in showing my work.	I need help in picking a strategy.

4-Point Sample

Name _____

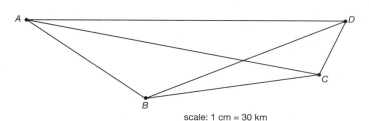

Distances
A to D = 11 cm
A to B = 5 cm
B to C = 6 cm
D to C = 2 cm
A to C = 10.5 cm

scale: 1 cm = 30 km

1. Write an equation to show how many kilometers a distance on the map actually is. Explain why your equation works.

   $y = 30x$ where y is the number of km in real life and x is the number of cm on the map.

   I multiplied the number of cm by 30 because the scale is 1 cm = 30 km. It is important to

   remember that the units change after you multiply and that y is the distance in km.

2. What is the difference between the distance from Town A to Town B and from Town A to Town C? Write an equation and give the answer.

   $\overline{AB} = 5$ cm and $\overline{AC} = 10.5$ cm. On the map, the difference is 5.5 cm. I used the equation
   I wrote in problem 1 and substituted 5.5 for x. So I had $y = 30 \times 5.5 = 165$ km.

3. Mr. Wong traveled from Town A to Town D and then to Town C. How many kilometers did he travel in all? Write an equation and give the answer.

   $\overline{AD} = 11$ cm and $\overline{DC} = 2$ cm. The total map distance is 13 cm. So $y = 30 \times 13 = 390$ km.
   So he traveled 390 km. The equation to solve this problem is $y = 30 \times (\overline{AD} + \overline{DC})$.

4. Formulate a problem about the map that goes with the equation $y = 330 - 180$.

   I used the equation from problem 1 and $330 = 30x$. So $x = 11$ cm. This is the distance of $\overline{AD}$.

   Also, $180 = 30x$. So $x = 6$ cm. This is the distance of $\overline{BC}$. One question I could ask is

   "How much farther is it to go from Town A to Town D than it is to go from Town B to Town C?"

5. Formulate a problem about the map. Write an equation to solve the problem. Solve the equation.

   What is the perimeter of the map?

   Perimeter $= 30 \times (\overline{AD} + \overline{DC} + \overline{BC} + \overline{AB}) = 30 \times 23 = 690$ km.

Saxon Math Course 2

3-Point Sample

Name _____

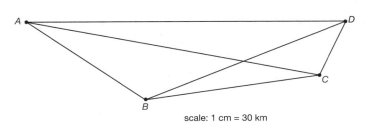

Distances
A to D = 11 cm
A to B = 5 cm
B to C = 6 cm
D to C = 2 cm
A to C = 10.5 cm

scale: 1 cm = 30 km

1. Write an equation to show how many kilometers a distance on the map actually is. Explain why your equation works.

   $y = 30x$. Every 1 cm equals 30 km. So if I have 2 cm, I multiply by 30 to get 60 km which is the answer.

2. What is the difference between the distance from Town A to Town B and from Town A to Town C? Write an equation and give the answer.

   $y = 315 - 150$, so $y = 165$ km.

3. Mr. Wong traveled from Town A to Town D and then to Town C. How many kilometers did he travel in all? Write an equation and give the answer.

   $y = 330 + 60$, so $y = 390$ km.

4. Formulate a problem about the map that goes with the equation $y = 330 - 180$.

   What is the difference between the distance from Town A to Town D and the distance from Town B to Town C?

5. Formulate a problem about the map. Write an equation to solve the problem. Solve the equation.

   What is the distance you will travel if you go from Town A to Town D and pass through Town C? $y = 315 + 60$, so $y = 375$ km.

     Saxon Math Course 2

2-Point Sample

Name _____

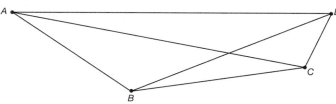

Distances
A to D = 11 cm
A to B = 5 cm
B to C = 6 cm
D to C = 2 cm
A to C = 10.5 cm

scale: 1 cm = 30 km

1. Write an equation to show how many kilometers a distance on the map actually is. Explain why your equation works.

30x. I multiplied thirty times x.

_____

_____

2. What is the difference between the distance from Town *A* to Town *B* and from Town *A* to Town *C*? Write an equation and give the answer.

y = 315 + 150 = 465 km.

3. Mr. Wong traveled from Town *A* to Town *D* and then to Town *C*. How many kilometers did he travel in all? Write an equation and give the answer.

11 + 2 = 13. He traveled 13 km.

4. Formulate a problem about the map that goes with the equation
y = 330 − 180.

John rode his bike from Town D to Town A and then rode to Town B.

How far did he ride?

_____

5. Formulate a problem about the map. Write an equation to solve the problem. Solve the equation.

How far is it from Town A to Town C? $\overline{AC}$ = 10.5,

y = 30 × 10.5 = 315.

_____

Saxon Math Course 2

1-Point Sample

Name _____   **Performance Activity 20**

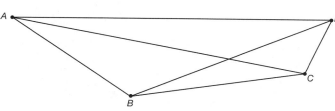

Distances
A to D = 11 cm
A to B = 5 cm
B to C = 6 cm
D to C = 2 cm
A to C = 10.5 cm

scale: 1 cm = 30 km

1. Write an equation to show how many kilometers a distance on the map actually is. Explain why your equation works.

x = 30 km. It works because they are equal.

2. What is the difference between the distance from Town *A* to Town *B* and from Town *A* to Town *C*? Write an equation and give the answer.

15.5

3. Mr. Wong traveled from Town *A* to Town *D* and then to Town *C*. How many kilometers did he travel in all? Write an equation and give the answer.

13 km

4. Formulate a problem about the map that goes with the equation
$y = 330 - 180$.

y = 150

5. Formulate a problem about the map. Write an equation to solve the problem. Solve the equation.

How many kilometers is B to D?

66
Saxon Math Course 2

Dear Parent or Guardian:

This year your child will be using a **Saxon Math** textbook. **Saxon** books are unlike traditional texts in which students are taught and expected to learn an entire mathematical concept in one day. Instead of practicing 30 problems of the same kind, **Saxon Math** builds mastery through daily practice of skills and concepts taught in earlier lessons.

Saxon textbooks divide concepts into small, easily grasped pieces called increments. A new increment is presented each day, and students work only a few problems each day involving the new material. The remaining homework problems cover previously introduced concepts. Thus, every assignment (and every test) is a review of material covered up to that point, providing students with the time and opportunity to understand and remember necessary concepts.

This is where your involvement is crucial. *It is essential that your child complete each day's assignment.* You can expect your child to complete three to five lessons per week with a test after every fifth lesson. Please ask to see your child's daily assignment, and encourage him or her to complete all the work. Students who complete all the daily assignments will have much to be proud of at test time, so you will have much to praise.

Some key words in the preface of your child's textbook are printed in boldface. They remind your child of the importance of the daily exercises. Those words are worth repeating here.

> *Solving these problems day after day is the secret to success. Work each problem in every practice set, in every problem set, and in every investigation. Do not skip problems. With honest effort you will experience success and true learning, which will stay with you and serve you well in the future.*

Learning mathematics is similar to learning a foreign language, a musical instrument, or an athletic skill. Becoming proficient requires long-term practice to develop and maintain mastery of the problem-solving skills needed for success in math-intensive disciplines.

Your child's experience in mathematics will be a direct result of his or her attitude and effort. A positive attitude and a commitment to long-term practice greatly improve the chances of your child progressing into higher-level mathematics courses and experiencing success in other fields that require mathematical understanding. Through our combined efforts your child can experience success at this level and learn the foundational skills needed for the next level.

Sincerely,

Estimados padres o tutores:

Este año su hijo(a) usará el libro de texto **Saxon** de matemáticas. Los libros de **Saxon** no son como los textos tradicionales, los cuales enseñan y esperan que los estudiantes aprendan todo un concepto matemático en un sólo día. En lugar de practicar 30 problemas del mismo tipo, las matemáticas de **Saxon** desarrollan destreza a través de la práctica de habilidades y conceptos enseñados en clases previas.

Los libros de texto de **Saxon** dividen los conceptos en unidades más pequeñas y más fáciles de comprender, llamadas incrementos. Un incremento nuevo es introducido cada día y diariamente los estudiantes resuelven sólo unos cuantos problemas que tratan sobre el material nuevo. El resto de los problemas de tarea cubren conceptos presentados previamente. De esta forma, cada tarea (y cada examen) es un repaso del material ya cubierto, lo cual da tiempo a los estudiantes y les ofrece la oportunidad de comprender y recordar conceptos necesarios.

Aquí es donde la participación de usted es crítica. *Es esencial que su hijo(a) termine la tarea de cada día.* Puede contar con que su hijo(a) cubrirá de 3 a 5 lecciones por semana y tomará un examen después de cada cinco lecciones. Por favor, pida a su hijo(a) que le muestre la tarea todos los días y aliéntelo(a) a que la haga en su totalidad. Los estudiantes que hayan terminado todas las tareas diarias se sentirán muy orgullosos del resultado de sus exámenes y ustedes tendrán mucha razón para felicitarlos.

Unas palabras claves del prólogo del libro de su hijo(a) están impresas en letra negrilla. Sirven para recordar a su hijo(a) la importancia de los ejercicios diarios. Vale la pena repetir esas palabras aquí.

> *Solucionar estos problemas día a día es el secreto del éxito. Resuelve cada problema en cada sección de práctica, en cada sección de problemas y en cada investigación. No te saltes problemas. A través del esfuerzo honesto obtendrás éxito y aprendizaje verdadero que mantendrás toda la vida y que te será muy útil en el futuro.*

El aprendizaje de matemáticas es similar al de un idioma extranjero, un instrumento musical, o una habilidad atlética. El llegar a ser competente requiere práctica a largo plazo para desarrollar y mantener el dominio de las destrezas necesarias para tener éxito en disciplinas que requieren muchas matemáticas.

La experiencia de su hijo(a) en matemáticas será el resultado directo de su actitud y su esfuerzo. Una actitud positiva y un compromiso a la práctica a largo plazo incrementan considerablemente la posibilidad de que su hijo(a) progrese hacia los cursos de matemáticas avanzadas y que tenga éxito en otras disciplinas que requieren compresión de matemáticas. A través de la combinación de nuestros esfuerzos, su hijo(a) puede lograr el éxito en este nivel y aprender los conocimientos fundamentales que necesitará para el siguiente nivel.

Sinceramente,

Name _____

Lesson _____

Show all necessary work.
Please be neat.

Power Up
☐ Facts
☐ Mental Math
☐ Problem Solving

Review
☐ Homework Check
☐ Error Correction

Instruction
☐ New Concept
☐ Practice Set
☐ Written Practice

Facts

Test:	Time:	Score:

Mental Math

a.	b.	c.	d.
e.	f.	g.	h.

Problem Solving

Strategies:
(check any you use)

☐ Make or use a table, chart or graph.
☐ Use logical reasoning.
☐ Act it out or make a model.
☐ Make an organized list.
☐ Write a number sentence or equation.
☐ Draw a picture or diagram.
☐ Guess and check.   ☐ Make it simpler.
☐ Work backwards.   ☐ Find a pattern.

Practice Set

a.	b.	c.
d.	e.	f.
g.	h.	i.
j.	k.	l.

Saxon Math Course 2

Name _____

Lesson _____

Written Practice Solutions

Show all necessary work.
Please be neat.

1.	2.	3.
4.	**5.**	**6.**
7.	**8.**	**9.**
10.	**11.**	**12.**
13.	**14.**	**15.**

Saxon Math Course 2

16.

17.

18.

19.

20.

21.

22.

23.

24.

25.

26.

27.

28.

29.

30.

Name _____

Lesson _____

Written Practice Solutions

Show all necessary work.
Please be neat.

1.	2.	3.
4.	5.	6.
7.	8.	9.
10.	11.	12.
13.	14.	15.

   Saxon Math Course 2

16.

17.

18.

19.

20.

21.

22.

23.

24.

25.

26.

27.

28.

29.

30.

Name _____

Power Up Facts	# Possible	Time and Score time / # correct									
A 40 Multiplication Facts	40										
B 20 Equations	20										
C 20 Improper Fractions and Mixed Numbers	20										
D 20 Fractions to Reduce	20										
E Circles	12										
F Lines, Angles, Polygons	12										
G + − × ÷ Fractions	16										
H Measurement Facts	30										
I Proportions	15										
J + − × ÷ Decimals	16										
K Powers and Roots	20										
L Fraction-Decimal-Percent Equivalents	24										
M Metric Conversions	22										
N + − × ÷ Mixed Numbers	16										
O Classifying Quadrilaterals and Triangles	8										
P + − × ÷ Integers	16										
Q Percent-Decimal-Fraction Equivalents	24										
R Area	8										
S Scientific Notation	12										
T Order of Operations	8										
U Two-Step Equations	12										
V + − × ÷ Algebraic Terms	16										
W Multiplying and Dividing in Scientific Notation	12										

Facts Multiply.

9 ×8	8 ×2	10 ×10	6 ×3	4 ×2	5 ×5	9 ×9	6 ×4	9 ×6	7 ×3
9 ×3	6 ×5	0 ×0	7 ×6	8 ×8	7 ×4	5 ×3	9 ×7	2 ×2	8 ×6
7 ×7	6 ×2	4 ×3	8 ×5	4 ×4	3 ×2	n ×0	8 ×4	6 ×6	9 ×2
8 ×3	5 ×4	n ×1	7 ×2	9 ×5	8 ×7	3 ×3	9 ×4	5 ×2	7 ×5

Mental Math

a.	b.	c.	d.
e.	f.	g.	h.

Problem Solving

Understand
What information am I given?
What am I asked to find or do?

- -

Plan
How can I use the information I am given?
Which strategy should I try?

- -

Solve
Did I follow the plan?
Did I show my work?
Did I write the answer?

- -

Check
Did I use the correct information?
Did I do what was asked?
Is my answer reasonable?

Name _____ Time _____

Facts   Solve each equation.

$a + 12 = 20$	$b - 8 = 10$	$5c = 40$	$\dfrac{d}{4} = 12$	$11 + e = 24$
$a =$	$b =$	$c =$	$d =$	$e =$
$25 - f = 10$	$10g = 60$	$\dfrac{24}{h} = 6$	$15 = j + 8$	$20 = k - 5$
$f =$	$g =$	$h =$	$j =$	$k =$
$30 = 6m$	$9 = \dfrac{n}{3}$	$18 = 6 + p$	$5 = 15 - q$	$36 = 4r$
$m =$	$n =$	$p =$	$q =$	$r =$
$2 = \dfrac{16}{s}$	$t + 8 = 12$	$u - 15 = 30$	$8v = 48$	$\dfrac{w}{3} = 6$
$s =$	$t =$	$u =$	$v =$	$w =$

Mental Math

a.	b.	c.	d.
e.	f.	g.	h.

Problem Solving

Understand
What information am I given?
What am I asked to find or do?

- -

Plan
How can I use the information I am given?
Which strategy should I try?

- -

Solve
Did I follow the plan?
Did I show my work?
Did I write the answer?

- -

Check
Did I use the correct information?
Did I do what was asked?
Is my answer reasonable?

       Saxon Math Course 2

Facts	Write each improper fraction as a whole number or mixed number.			
$\frac{5}{2} =$	$\frac{7}{4} =$	$\frac{12}{5} =$	$\frac{10}{3} =$	$\frac{15}{2} =$
$\frac{15}{5} =$	$\frac{11}{8} =$	$2\frac{3}{2} =$	$4\frac{5}{4} =$	$3\frac{7}{4} =$

Write each mixed number as an improper fraction.

$1\frac{1}{2} =$	$2\frac{2}{3} =$	$3\frac{3}{4} =$	$2\frac{1}{2} =$	$6\frac{2}{3} =$
$2\frac{3}{4} =$	$3\frac{1}{3} =$	$4\frac{1}{2} =$	$1\frac{7}{8} =$	$12\frac{1}{2} =$

Mental Math			
a.	**b.**	**c.**	**d.**
e.	**f.**	**g.**	**h.**

Problem Solving

Understand
What information am I given?
What am I asked to find or do?

- -

Plan
How can I use the information I am given?
Which strategy should I try?

- -

Solve
Did I follow the plan?
Did I show my work?
Did I write the answer?

- -

Check
Did I use the correct information?
Did I do what was asked?
Is my answer reasonable?

Facts	Reduce each fraction to lowest terms.			
$\frac{50}{100} =$	$\frac{4}{16} =$	$\frac{6}{8} =$	$\frac{8}{12} =$	$\frac{10}{100} =$
$\frac{8}{16} =$	$\frac{20}{100} =$	$\frac{3}{12} =$	$\frac{60}{100} =$	$\frac{9}{12} =$
$\frac{6}{9} =$	$\frac{90}{100} =$	$\frac{5}{10} =$	$\frac{12}{16} =$	$\frac{25}{100} =$
$\frac{4}{10} =$	$\frac{4}{6} =$	$\frac{75}{100} =$	$\frac{4}{12} =$	$\frac{6}{10} =$

Mental Math

a.	b.	c.	d.
e.	f.	g.	h.

Problem Solving

Understand

What information am I given?

What am I asked to find or do?

- -

Plan

How can I use the information I am given?

Which strategy should I try?

- -

Solve

Did I follow the plan?

Did I show my work?

Did I write the answer?

- -

Check

Did I use the correct information?

Did I do what was asked?

Is my answer reasonable?

Name _____ Time _____

Facts Write the word or words to complete each definition.

The distance around a circle is its	Every point on a circle is the same distance from its	The distance across a circle through it's center is its	The distance from a circle to it's center is its
_____.	_____.	_____.	_____.
Two or more circles with the same center are	A segment between two points on a circle is a	Part of a circumference is an	Part of a circle bounded by an arc and two radii is a
_____.	_____.	_____.	_____.
Half a circle is a	An angle whose vertex is the center of a circle is a	An angle whose vertex is on the circle whose sides include chords is an	A polygon whose vertices are on the circle and whose edges are within the circle is an
_____.	_____.	_____.	_____.

Mental Math

a.	b.	c.	d.
e.	f.	g.	h.

Problem Solving

Understand
What information am I given?
What am I asked to find or do?

- -

Plan
How can I use the information I am given?
Which strategy should I try?

- -

Solve
Did I follow the plan?
Did I show my work?
Did I write the answer?

- -

Check
Did I use the correct information?
Did I do what was asked?
Is my answer reasonable?

Facts   Name each figure illustrated.

1.	2.	3.	4.
5.	6.	7.	8.
9.	10.	11.	12. A polygon whose sides are equal in length and whose angles are equal in measure is a _____.

Mental Math

a.	b.	c.	d.
e.	f.	g.	h.

Problem Solving

Understand
What information am I given?
What am I asked to find or do?

Plan
How can I use the information I am given?
Which strategy should I try?

Solve
Did I follow the plan?
Did I show my work?
Did I write the answer?

Check
Did I use the correct information?
Did I do what was asked?
Is my answer reasonable?

               Saxon Math Course 2

Facts Simplify.

$\frac{2}{3} + \frac{2}{3} =$	$\frac{2}{3} - \frac{1}{3} =$	$\frac{2}{3} \times \frac{2}{3} =$	$\frac{2}{3} \div \frac{2}{3} =$
$\frac{3}{4} + \frac{1}{4} =$	$\frac{3}{4} - \frac{1}{4} =$	$\frac{3}{4} \times \frac{1}{4} =$	$\frac{3}{4} \div \frac{1}{4} =$
$\frac{2}{3} + \frac{1}{2} =$	$\frac{2}{3} - \frac{1}{2} =$	$\frac{2}{3} \times \frac{1}{2} =$	$\frac{2}{3} \div \frac{1}{2} =$
$\frac{3}{4} + \frac{2}{3} =$	$\frac{3}{4} - \frac{2}{3} =$	$\frac{3}{4} \times \frac{2}{3} =$	$\frac{3}{4} \div \frac{2}{3} =$

Mental Math

a.	b.	c.	d.
e.	f.	g.	h.

Problem Solving

Understand
What information am I given?
What am I asked to find or do?

Plan
How can I use the information I am given?
Which strategy should I try?

Solve
Did I follow the plan?
Did I show my work?
Did I write the answer?

Check
Did I use the correct information?
Did I do what was asked?
Is my answer reasonable?

Name _____ Time _____

Facts   Write the number that completes each equivalent measure.

1. 1 foot	= _____	inches
2. 1 yard	= _____	inches
3. 1 yard	= _____	feet
4. 1 mile	= _____	feet

5. 1 centimeter	= _____	millimeters
6. 1 meter	= _____	millimeters
7. 1 meter	= _____	centimeters
8. 1 kilometer	= _____	meters
9. 1 inch	= _____	centimeters

10. 1 pound	= _____	ounces
11. 1 ton	= _____	pounds
12. 1 gram	= _____	milligrams
13. 1 kilogram	= _____	grams
14. 1 metric ton	= _____	kilograms

15. 1 kilogram	≈ _____	pounds

16. 1 pint	= _____	ounces
17. 1 pint	= _____	cups
18. 1 quart	= _____	pints
19. 1 gallon	= _____	quarts

20. 1 liter	= _____	milliliters

21–24. 1 milliliter of water has a volume of _____ and a mass of _____ .
One liter of water has a volume of _____ cm^3 and a mass of _____ kg.

25–26. Water freezes at _____ °F and _____ °C.

27–28. Water boils at _____ °F and _____ °C.

29–30. Normal body temperature is _____ °F and _____ °C.

Mental Math

a.	b.	c.	d.
e.	f.	g.	h.

Problem Solving

Understand
What information am I given?
What am I asked to find or do?

Plan
How can I use the information I am given?
Which strategy should I try?

Solve
Did I follow the plan?
Did I show my work?
Did I write the answer?

Check
Did I use the correct information?
Did I do what was asked?
Is my answer reasonable?

Facts Find the number that completes each proportion.

$\dfrac{3}{4} = \dfrac{a}{12}$	$\dfrac{3}{4} = \dfrac{12}{b}$	$\dfrac{c}{5} = \dfrac{12}{20}$	$\dfrac{2}{d} = \dfrac{12}{24}$	$\dfrac{8}{12} = \dfrac{4}{e}$
$\dfrac{f}{10} = \dfrac{10}{5}$	$\dfrac{5}{g} = \dfrac{25}{100}$	$\dfrac{10}{100} = \dfrac{5}{h}$	$\dfrac{8}{4} = \dfrac{j}{16}$	$\dfrac{24}{k} = \dfrac{8}{6}$
$\dfrac{9}{12} = \dfrac{36}{m}$	$\dfrac{50}{100} = \dfrac{w}{30}$	$\dfrac{3}{9} = \dfrac{5}{p}$	$\dfrac{q}{60} = \dfrac{15}{20}$	$\dfrac{2}{5} = \dfrac{r}{100}$

Mental Math

a.	**b.**	**c.**	**d.**
e.	**f.**	**g.**	**h.**

Problem Solving

Understand
What information am I given?
What am I asked to find or do?

Plan
How can I use the information I am given?
Which strategy should I try?

Solve
Did I follow the plan?
Did I show my work?
Did I write the answer?

Check
Did I use the correct information?
Did I do what was asked?
Is my answer reasonable?

Facts   Simplify.

0.8 + 0.4 =	0.8 − 0.4 =	0.8 × 0.4 =	0.8 ÷ 0.4 =
1.2 + 0.4 =	1.2 − 0.4 =	1.2 × 0.4 =	1.2 ÷ 0.4 =
6 + 0.3 =	6 − 0.3 =	6 × 0.3 =	6 ÷ 0.3 =
1.2 + 4 =	0.01 − 0.01 =	0.3 × 0.3 =	0.12 ÷ 4 =

Mental Math

a.	**b.**	**c.**	**d.**
e.	**f.**	**g.**	**h.**

Problem Solving

Understand
What information am I given?
What am I asked to find or do?

Plan
How can I use the information I am given?
Which strategy should I try?

Solve
Did I follow the plan?
Did I show my work?
Did I write the answer?

Check
Did I use the correct information?
Did I do what was asked?
Is my answer reasonable?

Facts   Simplify each power or root.

$\sqrt{100} =$	$\sqrt{16} =$	$\sqrt{81} =$	$\sqrt{4} =$	$\sqrt{144} =$
$\sqrt{64} =$	$\sqrt{49} =$	$\sqrt{25} =$	$\sqrt{9} =$	$\sqrt{36} =$
$8^2 =$	$5^2 =$	$3^2 =$	$12^2 =$	$10^2 =$
$7^2 =$	$2^3 =$	$3^3 =$	$10^3 =$	$5^3 =$

Mental Math

a.	b.	c.	d.
e.	f.	g.	h.

Problem Solving

Understand
What information am I given?
What am I asked to find or do?

Plan
How can I use the information I am given?
Which strategy should I try?

Solve
Did I follow the plan?
Did I show my work?
Did I write the answer?

Check
Did I use the correct information?
Did I do what was asked?
Is my answer reasonable?

Facts — Write the equivalent decimal and percent for each fraction.

Fraction	Decimal	Percent	Fraction	Decimal	Percent
$\frac{1}{2}$			$\frac{1}{8}$		
$\frac{1}{3}$			$\frac{1}{10}$		
$\frac{2}{3}$			$\frac{3}{10}$		
$\frac{1}{4}$			$\frac{9}{10}$		
$\frac{3}{4}$			$\frac{1}{100}$		
$\frac{1}{5}$			$1\frac{1}{2}$		

Mental Math

a.	b.	c.	d.
e.	f.	g.	h.

Problem Solving

Understand
What information am I given?
What am I asked to find or do?

Plan
How can I use the information I am given?
Which strategy should I try?

Solve
Did I follow the plan?
Did I show my work?
Did I write the answer?

Check
Did I use the correct information?
Did I do what was asked?
Is my answer reasonable?

Facts   Write the number for each conversion or factor.

					Prefix	Factor
1. 2 m = _____ cm	9. 2 L = _____ mL	17.	kilo-			
2. 1.5 km = _____ m	10. 250 mL = _____ L	18.	hecto-			
3. 2.54 cm = _____ mm	11. 4 kg = _____ g	19.	deka-			
4. 125 cm = _____ m	12. 2.5 g = _____ mg		(unit)			
5. 10 km = _____ m	13. 500 mg = _____ g	20.	deci-			
6. 5000 m = _____ km	14. 0.5 kg = _____ g	21.	centi-			
7. 50 cm = _____ m	15–16. Two liters of water have a volume of _____ cm³	22.	milli-			
8. 50 cm = _____ mm	and a mass of ___ kg.					

1. 2 m = _____ cm

2. 1.5 km = _____ m

3. 2.54 cm = _____ mm

4. 125 cm = _____ m

5. 10 km = _____ m

6. 5000 m = _____ km

7. 50 cm = _____ m

8. 50 cm = _____ mm

9. 2 L = _____ mL

10. 250 mL = _____ L

11. 4 kg = _____ g

12. 2.5 g = _____ mg

13. 500 mg = _____ g

14. 0.5 kg = _____ g

15–16. Two liters of water have a volume of _____ cm³ and a mass of ___ kg.

	Prefix	Factor
17.	kilo-	
18.	hecto-	
19.	deka-	
	(unit)	
20.	deci-	
21.	centi-	
22.	milli-	

Mental Math

a.	**b.**	**c.**	**d.**
e.	**f.**	**g.**	**h.**

Problem Solving

Understand
What information am I given?
What am I asked to find or do?

Plan
How can I use the information I am given?
Which strategy should I try?

Solve
Did I follow the plan?
Did I show my work?
Did I write the answer?

Check
Did I use the correct information?
Did I do what was asked?
Is my answer reasonable?

Facts	Simplify. Reduce the answers if possible.		
$3 + 1\frac{2}{3} =$	$3 - 1\frac{2}{3} =$	$3 \times 1\frac{2}{3} =$	$3 \div 1\frac{2}{3} =$
$1\frac{2}{3} + 1\frac{1}{2} =$	$1\frac{2}{3} - 1\frac{1}{2} =$	$1\frac{2}{3} \times 1\frac{1}{2} =$	$1\frac{2}{3} \div 1\frac{1}{2} =$
$2\frac{1}{2} + 1\frac{2}{3} =$	$2\frac{1}{2} - 1\frac{2}{3} =$	$2\frac{1}{2} \times 1\frac{2}{3} =$	$2\frac{1}{2} \div 1\frac{2}{3} =$
$4\frac{1}{2} + 2\frac{1}{4} =$	$4\frac{1}{2} - 2\frac{1}{4} =$	$4\frac{1}{2} \times 2\frac{1}{4} =$	$4\frac{1}{2} \div 2\frac{1}{4} =$

Mental Math			
a.	**b.**	**c.**	**d.**
e.	**f.**	**g.**	**h.**

Problem Solving

Understand
What information am I given?
What am I asked to find or do?

Plan
How can I use the information I am given?
Which strategy should I try?

Solve
Did I follow the plan?
Did I show my work?
Did I write the answer?

Check
Did I use the correct information?
Did I do what was asked?
Is my answer reasonable?

Facts   Select from the words below to describe each figure.

1.	2.	3.	4.
_____	_____	_____	_____
_____	_____	_____	_____
_____	_____	_____	_____

5.	6.	7.	8.
_____	_____	_____	_____
_____	_____	_____	_____

kite	rectangle	isosceles triangle	right triangle
trapezoid	rhombus	scalene triangle	acute triangle
parallelogram	square	equilateral triangle	obtuse triangle

Mental Math

a.	b.	c.	d.
e.	f.	g.	h.

Problem Solving

Understand
What information am I given?
What am I asked to find or do?

Plan
How can I use the information I am given?
Which strategy should I try?

Solve
Did I follow the plan?
Did I show my work?
Did I write the answer?

Check
Did I use the correct information?
Did I do what was asked?
Is my answer reasonable?

Facts   Simplify.

(−8) + (−2) =	(−8) − (−2) =	(−8)(−2) =	$\frac{-8}{-2} =$
(−9) + (+3) =	(−9) − (+3) =	(−9)(+3) =	$\frac{-9}{+3} =$
12 + (−2) =	12 − (−2) =	(12)(−2) =	$\frac{12}{-2} =$
(−4) + (−3) + (−2) =	(−4) − (−3) − (−2) =	(−4)(−3)(−2) =	$\frac{(-4)(-3)}{(-2)} =$

Mental Math

a.	b.	c.	d.
e.	f.	g.	h.

Problem Solving

Understand
What information am I given?
What am I asked to find or do?

- -

Plan
How can I use the information I am given?
Which strategy should I try?

- -

Solve
Did I follow the plan?
Did I show my work?
Did I write the answer?

- -

Check
Did I use the correct information?
Did I do what was asked?
Is my answer reasonable?

Facts Write the equivalent decimal and fraction for each percent.

Percent	Decimal	Fraction	Percent	Decimal	Fraction
10%			$33\frac{1}{3}\%$		
90%			20%		
5%			75%		
$12\frac{1}{2}\%$			$66\frac{2}{3}\%$		
50%			1%		
25%			250%		

Mental Math

a.	b.	c.	d.
e.	f.	g.	h.

Problem Solving

Understand
What information am I given?
What am I asked to find or do?

Plan
How can I use the information I am given?
Which strategy should I try?

Solve
Did I follow the plan?
Did I show my work?
Did I write the answer?

Check
Did I use the correct information?
Did I do what was asked?
Is my answer reasonable?

Name _____ Time _____

Find the area of each figure. Angles that look like
Facts right angles are right angles.

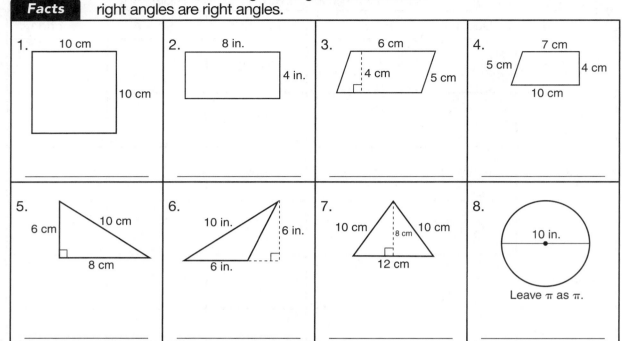

1. 10 cm
10 cm

2. 8 in.
4 in.

3. 6 cm
4 cm
5 cm

4. 7 cm
5 cm
4 cm
10 cm

5. 6 cm
10 cm
8 cm

6. 10 in.
6 in.
6 in.

7. 10 cm
8 cm
10 cm
12 cm

8. 10 in.

Leave π as π.

Mental Math

a.	b.	c.	d.
e.	f.	g.	h.

Problem Solving

Understand
What information am I given?
What am I asked to find or do?

- -

Plan
How can I use the information I am given?
Which strategy should I try?

- -

Solve
Did I follow the plan?
Did I show my work?
Did I write the answer?

- -

Check
Did I use the correct information?
Did I do what was asked?
Is my answer reasonable?

 Saxon Math Course 2

Facts Write each number in scientific notation.

186,000 =	0.0005 =	30,500,000 =
2.5 billion =	12 million =	$\dfrac{1}{1,000,000} =$

Write each number in standard form.

$1 \times 10^6 =$	$1 \times 10^{-6} =$	$2.4 \times 10^4 =$
$5 \times 10^{-4} =$	$4.75 \times 10^5 =$	$2.5 \times 10^{-3} =$

Mental Math

a.	b.	c.	d.
e.	f.	g.	h.

Problem Solving

Understand
What information am I given?
What am I asked to find or do?

- -

Plan
How can I use the information I am given?
Which strategy should I try?

- -

Solve
Did I follow the plan?
Did I show my work?
Did I write the answer?

- -

Check
Did I use the correct information?
Did I do what was asked?
Is my answer reasonable?

Facts   Simplify.

$6 + 6 \times 6 - 6 \div 6 =$	$3^2 + \sqrt{4} + 5(6) - 7 + 8 =$
$4 + 2(3 + 5) - 6 \div 2 =$	$2 + 2[3 + 4(7 - 5)] =$
$\sqrt{1^3 + 2^3 + 3^3} =$	$\dfrac{4 + 3(7 - 5)}{6 - (5 - 4)} =$
$(-3)(-3) + (-3) - (-3) =$	$\dfrac{3(-3) - (-3)(-3)}{(-3) - (3)(-3)} =$

Mental Math

a.	b.	c.	d.
e.	f.	g.	h.

Problem Solving

Understand
What information am I given?
What am I asked to find or do?

- -

Plan
How can I use the information I am given?
Which strategy should I try?

- -

Solve
Did I follow the plan?
Did I show my work?
Did I write the answer?

- -

Check
Did I use the correct information?
Did I do what was asked?
Is my answer reasonable?

Saxon Math Course 2

Facts   Complete each step to solve each equation.

$2x + 5 = 45$	$3y + 4 = 22$	$5n - 3 = 12$	$3m - 7 = 14$
$2x =$	$3y =$	$5n =$	$3m =$
$x =$	$y =$	$n =$	$m =$
$15 = 3a - 6$	$24 = 2w + 6$	$-2x + 9 = 23$	$20 - 3y = 2$
$= 3a$	$= 2w$	$-2x =$	$-3y =$
$= a$	$= w$	$x =$	$y =$
$\frac{1}{2}m + 6 = 18$	$\frac{3}{4}n - 12 = 12$	$3y + 1.5 = 6$	$0.5w - 1.5 = 4.5$
$\frac{1}{2}m =$	$\frac{3}{4}n =$	$3y =$	$0.5w =$
$m =$	$n =$	$y =$	$w =$

Mental Math

a.	**b.**	**c.**	**d.**
e.	**f.**	**g.**	**h.**

Problem Solving

Understand
What information am I given?
What am I asked to find or do?

- -

Plan
How can I use the information I am given?
Which strategy should I try?

- -

Solve
Did I follow the plan?
Did I show my work?
Did I write the answer?

- -

Check
Did I use the correct information?
Did I do what was asked?
Is my answer reasonable?

Name _____ Time _____

Facts   Solve each equation.

$6x + 2x =$	$6x - 2x =$	$(6x)(2x) =$	$\dfrac{6x}{2x} =$
$9xy + 3xy =$	$9xy - 3xy =$	$(9xy)(3xy) =$	$\dfrac{9xy}{3xy} =$
$x + y + x =$	$x + y - x =$	$(x)(y)(-x) =$	$\dfrac{xy}{x} =$
$3x + x + 3 =$	$3x - x - 3 =$	$(3x)(-x)(-3) =$	$\dfrac{(2x)(8xy)}{4y} =$

Mental Math

a.	b.	c.	d.
e.	f.	g.	h.

Problem Solving

Understand
What information am I given?
What am I asked to find or do?

- -

Plan
How can I use the information I am given?
Which strategy should I try?

- -

Solve
Did I follow the plan?
Did I show my work?
Did I write the answer?

- -

Check
Did I use the correct information?
Did I do what was asked?
Is my answer reasonable?

     Saxon Math Course 2

Facts   Simplify. Write each answer in scientific notation.

$(1 \times 10^6)(1 \times 10^6) =$	$(3 \times 10^3)(3 \times 10^3) =$	$(4 \times 10^{-5})(2 \times 10^{-6}) =$
$(5 \times 10^5)(5 \times 10^5) =$	$(6 \times 10^{-3})(7 \times 10^{-4}) =$	$(3 \times 10^6)(2 \times 10^{-4}) =$
$\dfrac{8 \times 10^8}{2 \times 10^2} =$	$\dfrac{5 \times 10^6}{2 \times 10^3} =$	$\dfrac{9 \times 10^3}{3 \times 10^8} =$
$\dfrac{2 \times 10^6}{4 \times 10^2} =$	$\dfrac{1 \times 10^{-3}}{4 \times 10^8} =$	$\dfrac{8 \times 10^{-8}}{2 \times 10^{-2}} =$

Mental Math

a.	b.	c.	d.
e.	f.	g.	h.

Problem Solving

Understand
What information am I given?
What am I asked to find or do?

Plan
How can I use the information I am given?
Which strategy should I try?

Solve
Did I follow the plan?
Did I show my work?
Did I write the answer?

Check
Did I use the correct information?
Did I do what was asked?
Is my answer reasonable?

Add.

3 + 2	8 + 3	2 + 1	5 + 6	2 + 9	4 + 8	8 + 0	3 + 9	1 + 0	6 + 3
7 + 3	1 + 6	4 + 7	0 + 3	6 + 4	5 + 5	3 + 1	7 + 2	8 + 5	2 + 5
4 + 0	5 + 7	1 + 1	5 + 4	2 + 8	7 + 1	4 + 6	0 + 2	6 + 5	4 + 9
8 + 6	0 + 4	5 + 8	7 + 4	1 + 7	6 + 6	4 + 1	8 + 2	2 + 4	6 + 0
9 + 1	8 + 8	2 + 2	4 + 5	6 + 2	0 + 0	5 + 9	3 + 3	8 + 1	2 + 7
4 + 4	7 + 5	0 + 1	8 + 7	3 + 4	7 + 9	1 + 2	6 + 7	0 + 8	9 + 2
0 + 9	8 + 9	7 + 6	1 + 3	6 + 8	2 + 0	8 + 4	3 + 5	9 + 8	5 + 0
9 + 3	2 + 6	3 + 0	6 + 1	3 + 6	5 + 2	0 + 5	6 + 9	1 + 8	9 + 6
4 + 3	9 + 9	0 + 7	9 + 4	7 + 7	1 + 4	3 + 7	7 + 0	2 + 3	5 + 1
9 + 5	1 + 5	9 + 0	3 + 8	1 + 9	5 + 3	4 + 2	9 + 7	0 + 6	7 + 8

Saxon Math Course 2

Name _____ Time _____

Subtract.

16 − 9	7 − 1	18 − 9	11 − 3	13 − 7	8 − 2	11 − 5	5 − 0	17 − 9	6 − 1
10 − 9	6 − 2	13 − 9	4 − 0	10 − 5	5 − 1	10 − 3	12 − 6	10 − 1	6 − 4
7 − 2	14 − 7	8 − 1	11 − 6	3 − 3	16 − 7	5 − 2	12 − 4	3 − 0	11 − 7
17 − 8	6 − 0	10 − 6	4 − 1	9 − 5	9 − 0	5 − 4	12 − 5	4 − 2	9 − 3
12 − 3	16 − 8	9 − 1	15 − 6	11 − 4	13 − 5	1 − 0	8 − 5	9 − 6	11 − 2
7 − 0	10 − 8	6 − 3	14 − 5	3 − 1	8 − 6	4 − 4	11 − 8	3 − 2	15 − 9
13 − 8	7 − 4	10 − 7	0 − 0	12 − 8	5 − 5	4 − 3	8 − 7	7 − 3	7 − 6
5 − 3	7 − 5	2 − 1	6 − 6	8 − 4	2 − 2	13 − 6	15 − 8	2 − 0	13 − 9
1 − 1	11 − 9	10 − 4	9 − 2	14 − 6	8 − 0	9 − 4	10 − 2	6 − 5	8 − 3
7 − 7	14 − 8	12 − 9	9 − 8	12 − 7	9 − 9	15 − 7	8 − 8	14 − 9	9 − 7

Multiply.

9 ×9	3 ×5	8 ×5	2 ×6	4 ×7	0 ×3	7 ×2	1 ×5	7 ×8	4 ×0
3 ×4	5 ×9	0 ×2	7 ×3	4 ×1	2 ×7	6 ×3	5 ×4	1 ×0	9 ×2
1 ×1	9 ×0	2 ×8	6 ×4	0 ×7	8 ×1	3 ×3	4 ×8	9 ×3	2 ×0
4 ×9	7 ×0	1 ×2	8 ×4	6 ×5	2 ×9	9 ×4	0 ×1	7 ×4	5 ×8
0 ×8	4 ×2	9 ×8	3 ×6	5 ×5	1 ×6	5 ×0	6 ×6	2 ×1	7 ×9
9 ×1	2 ×2	5 ×1	4 ×3	0 ×0	8 ×9	3 ×7	9 ×7	1 ×7	6 ×0
5 ×6	7 ×5	3 ×0	8 ×8	1 ×3	8 ×3	5 ×2	0 ×4	9 ×5	6 ×7
2 ×3	8 ×6	0 ×5	6 ×1	3 ×8	7 ×6	1 ×8	9 ×6	4 ×4	5 ×3
7 ×7	1 ×4	6 ×2	4 ×5	2 ×4	8 ×0	3 ×1	6 ×8	0 ×9	8 ×7
3 ×2	4 ×6	1 ×9	5 ×7	8 ×2	0 ×6	7 ×1	2 ×5	6 ×9	3 ×9

Divide.

7)21	2)10	6)42	1)3	4)24	3)6	9)54	6)18	4)0	5)30
4)32	8)56	1)0	6)12	3)18	9)72	5)15	2)8	7)42	6)36
6)0	5)10	9)9	2)6	7)63	4)16	8)48	1)2	5)35	3)21
2)18	6)6	3)15	8)40	2)0	5)20	9)27	1)8	4)4	7)35
4)20	9)63	1)4	7)14	3)3	8)24	5)0	6)24	8)8	2)16
5)5	8)64	3)0	4)28	7)49	2)4	9)81	3)12	6)30	1)5
8)32	1)1	9)36	3)27	2)14	5)25	6)48	8)0	7)28	4)36
2)12	5)45	1)7	4)8	7)0	8)16	3)24	9)45	1)9	6)54
7)56	9)0	8)72	2)2	5)40	3)9	9)18	1)6	4)12	7)7

To help produce the exhibit titled *Into the Sky and Into the Earth*, the Museum Director has asked you to check the accuracy of the statements made in the exhibit. Later your task will be to help plan a budget.

Use the information in the Museum Exhibit Data Charts to complete the exercises.

1. Decide if each statement is true or false and explain why. If the statement is false, rewrite it to make it true.

   a. The difference between the height of Denali and the height of Vinson Massif is 4297 feet.

   _____

   _____

   b. The greatest depth in Carlsbad Caverns is a little more than twice the greatest depth in Mammoth Caves.

   _____

   _____

   c. The caves in order from shortest length to longest are:
   Carlsbad Caverns, Mammoth Caves, Neff Canyon, Ellison's Cave

   _____

   _____

   _____

2. The length of Ellison's Cave is about what fraction of the length of Carlsbad Caverns? Explain your thinking.

_____

_____

_____

3. Look at the data in the two tables about mountains and caves. Write two conclusions that you can put on signs for the walls of the museum exhibit. Explain how you know each conclusion is correct.

_____

_____

_____

_____

4. **Extension** The money that has been spent on this exhibit so far is given in a table on the Data Chart page. The total budget for the exhibit is $23,000. The Museum Director wants to use the money that has not been spent for a party to celebrate the opening of the exhibit.

   a. How much money can the Director spend on the party?

   _____

   b. The Director asks you to help budget money for the party according to expense ratios she provided. $\frac{Music}{Total} = \frac{1}{4}$ Food $\leq \frac{1}{3}$ Decorations $\leq \frac{1}{4}$ Invitations $\leq \frac{1}{6}$. Make a plan for a party to show how you will spend the money.

   _____

   _____

   _____

     Saxon Math Course 2

Museum Exhibit Data Charts

Height of Tallest Mountain in Each of Six Continents

Name and Location of Mountain	Height
Aconcagua, Argentina Continent: South America	22,840 feet
Denali, Alaska Continent: North America	20,320 feet
Kilimanjaro, Tanzania Continent: Africa	19,339 feet
Mount Everest, Nepal/Tibet Continent: Asia	29,029 feet
Vinson Massif, Ellsworth Range Continent: Antarctica	16,023 feet

Caves and Caverns in the United States

Name and Location of Cave	Length of Caverns	Greatest Depth
Carlsbad Caverns, New Mexico	23 miles	1014 feet
Ellison's Cave, Georgia	64,030 feet	1063 feet
Mammoth Caves, Kentucky	348 miles	450 feet
Neff Canyon, Utah	1700 feet	1189 feet

Money Spent: *Into the Sky and Into the Earth Exhibit*

Category	Money Spent
Materials	$5374
Labor	$12,956
Advertising	$2985

Name _____

You are helping the Centerville mayor publish information about the town on a Web site. However, you have run into a problem. There are three statements about Centerville and three diagrams but there is nothing that says which diagram goes with which statement. The mayor is out of town so you must decide.

Statement 1: $\frac{3}{5}$ of the city garden is devoted to growing vegetables.

Statement 2: The library is located $\frac{3}{5}$ of the way along the road from City Hall to the school.

Statement 3: Three out of every five people in Centerville use the library.

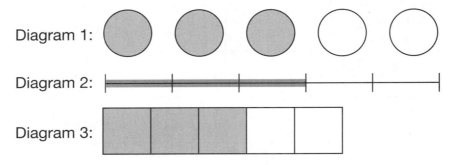

Diagram 1:

Diagram 2:

Diagram 3:

Decide which diagram best represents each statement. Explain how you made each decision.

1. _____

_____

_____

2. _____

_____

_____

3. _____

_____

_____

Last season, the football team won its twentieth Division Championship title. For a celebration at halftime at this season's Homecoming game, you have been asked to help design a "flag" that covers most of the playing field, using vinyl "tiles." The tiles must meet these requirements:

- All tiles must be square. You must use whole tiles.
- You must have enough tiles to cover an area of the football field that is 99 yards long by 54 yards wide.
- Tiles must be either black or white. You must use 20 black tiles to form letters or symbols representing "20," for the number of championships won.
- The flag design must be symmetrical.

1. Use the grid below to show how you would arrange the tiles. Show all the dimensions and indicate the size of the tiles you will be using.

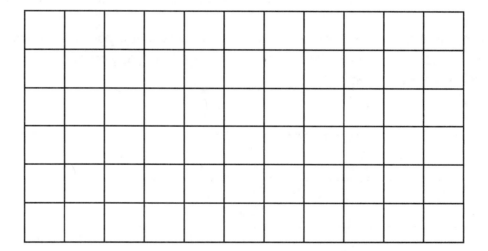

2. What is the perimeter of the flag in feet?

_____

3. Describe how your design is symmetrical.

_____

4. How many tiles do you need to cover the flag's area? Use the number of tiles in the length and width of the flag and the square area of each tile to calculate the total area covered by the flag.

_____

The table below shows the prices for vinyl from different suppliers.

Supplier	Price
Sign and banner company	$0.81 per sq. yd (any color)
Discount vinyl retailer	$0.57 per sq. yd white $1.38 per sq. yd black

5. Compare the cost of buying vinyl from the two suppliers, based on the total number and color of tiles your design requires.

_____

_____

6. To replace tiles that were damaged during rehearsal, you need to order vinyl for 10 more white tiles. Which supplier would you buy from to minimize cost? Justify your answer.

_____

_____

_____

_____

Name _____

Use an example to disprove each of these statements.

1. You can apply the Commutative Property to subtraction.

_____

_____

2. You can apply the Associative Property to subtraction.

_____

_____

3. If the numerator of a fraction is divisible by 5 and the denominator is divisible by 6, the fraction cannot be reduced.

_____

_____

4. There are no prime numbers greater than 100.

_____

_____

5. The following mathematical statement is true for positive numbers and false for negative numbers. If $a > b$ and $a - b = c$, then $c < a$.

a. Write an example using positive numbers to illustrate the truth of the statement.

_____

b. Write an example using negative numbers to illustrate that the statement is not true for negative numbers.

_____

Name _____

Your task at The Bread Bakery, is to prepare ingredients for making the bread. Today you are going to pre-measure the flour to help the baker make whole wheat bread and rye bread.

1. It takes $1\frac{3}{4}$ cups of rye flour to make 1 loaf of rye bread. Complete the table to show how much rye flour the baker needs to make different numbers of loaves.

Number of Loaves of Rye Bread	3	6	9	12	15	18	21
Number of Cups of Flour	$5\frac{1}{4}$						

2. There are 34 cups of flour in a ten-pound bag of flour. How many bags of flour does the baker need to make 21 loaves of rye bread? Explain your thinking.

_____

_____

_____

3. **a.** Write a rule that shows how much flour you should pre-measure for different numbers of loaves. Use *x* for the number of loaves and *y* for the number of cups of flour.

_____

   b. Use the equation to find out how many cups of flour are needed to make 30 loaves.

_____

_____

 Saxon Math Course 2

Do exercises **4–6** to find out how much whole wheat flour you should measure to make whole wheat bread.

4. It takes $8\frac{1}{3}$ cups of whole wheat flour to make 4 loaves of whole wheat bread. Complete the table to show how much flour you should measure to make different numbers of loaves.

Number of Loaves of Bread	4	8	12	16	20	24	28
Number of Cups of Whole Wheat Flour	$8\frac{1}{3}$						

5. There are 34 cups of flour in a ten-pound bag of whole wheat flour. How many bags of whole wheat flour do you need to set aside to make 20 loaves of whole wheat bread? Explain your thinking.

_____

_____

_____

6. How many cups of whole wheat flour do you need to make 30 loaves of whole wheat bread? Explain how you found your answer.

_____

_____

_____

_____

As President of the Bird Club, you are in charge of setting up the annual exhibit. This year's exhibit is on very large and very small birds. You want to put the data below into a representational form.

Hours Worked by Bird Club Members to Set Up Show

Member A: 5 hours	Member A: 3 hours
Member B: 6 hours	Member B: 11 hours
Member C: 10 hours	Member C: 5 hours
Member D: 5 hours	Member D: 5 hours
Member E: 2 hours	Member E: 6 hours

Eagles and Hummingbirds

Eagles	Hummingbirds
Bald Eagle, United States Bateleur Eagle, Africa Crested Serpent Eagle, Africa	Blue-throated Hummingbird, United States Cinnamon Hummingbird, Mexico Emerald-chinned Hummingbird, Mexico Ruby-throated Hummingbird, United States Violet-crowned Hummingbird, United States

1. Would you choose a line plot or a Venn diagram to show the spread of the hours worked by the volunteers? Draw the representation and explain your choice.

   _____

   _____

2. Would you choose a line plot or a Venn diagram to show the criteria below in one representation. Draw the representation and explain your choice.

   • the birds in the exhibit that are eagles

   • the birds in the exhibit that are hummingbirds

   • the birds that live in the United States

   • the birds that don't live in the United States

   _____

   _____

The Sanchez Survey Company takes surveys for companies. They recently did a survey in a town of 10,000 people to find out if the citizens of the town would prefer a swimming pool, tennis court, or baseball field in the town's new recreation park.

1. They asked 5 people and all 5 people wanted a swimming pool. If they make a prediction based on this data, what might they conclude?

   _____

   _____

2. Then they asked 1000 people about their preferences and found that:
   231 people wanted a swimming pool
   496 people wanted a baseball field, and
   273 people wanted a tennis court.
   If they make their prediction based on this data, what might they conclude?
   Explain your thinking.

   _____

   _____

   _____

   _____

3. Finally the town took a vote. The results of the vote were that 2156 people wanted a swimming pool, 5045 people wanted a baseball field, and 2799 people wanted a tennis court. What did most of the people in the town want?

   _____

4. Did the survey company get a result that was closer to the actual preferences with the sample of 5 or with the sample of 1000? Explain why or why not.

   _____

   _____

   _____

Answer exercise **5**.

5. Take a survey of four people in your class. Ask:

a. Which of these three sports, basketball, baseball, or football do you like best? Record the results.

_____

b. Based on your results, what would you predict is the favorite sport of most of the students in your class?

_____

c. Now ask six more people in your class which of the three sports they like the best. Record the results, including the sample of four people from 5a.

_____

_____

d. Based on your sample of 10 responses, what would you predict is the **least** favorite sport of most of the students in your class?

_____

e. Now ask everyone else in your class which of the three sports they like the best. Combine their responses with those gathered before and record the results.

_____

_____

f. Compare the result from the sample of four and the sample of ten, to the results for the class. Which sample size gave you the best idea about favorite sports? Why?

_____

_____

Use an example to disprove each of these statements.

1. If you double the side of a square you double the area.

_____

_____

2. If two different rectangles have the same area, they will always have the same perimeter.

_____

_____

3. If one angle of a triangle measures 100°, the other two angles in the triangle must have a sum that is greater than 80°.

_____

_____

4. Write a mathematical statement that is true for right triangles and false for triangles that are not right triangles. Use examples and non-examples.

_____

_____

_____

As the assistant to the Director of a Web site on distance running, your task is to organize some of the data from the 2005 Boston Marathon. The table on Data Sheet **9B** shows the results of the 38 women who ran the 2005 Boston Marathon in under 3 hours. However, the table does not tell the whole story. For example, the first place woman ran about 34 minutes faster than the last woman on the sheet. In addition, fewer than half of the women on the sheet ran faster than 2 hours and 50 minutes. Your task is to make this data clear and meaningful. The Director of the Web site wants to see the runners grouped in time increments to demonstrate the frequency of certain race times among the women.

1. Complete a frequency table to represent the data in the chart. This table should show the number of runners that fall within time ranges you specify. Think about what would be a good range of race times to use for your frequency table.

Frequency Table	
Time Range	**Number of Finishers**

2. Use the data from your frequency table to make a histogram that shows the time ranges you specified and the frequency in which those race times occurred.

2005 Boston Marathon
Women Finishers Under 3 Hours

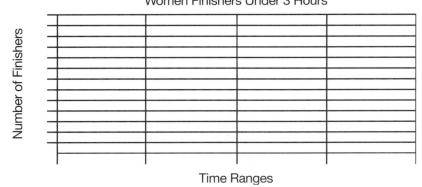

Time Ranges

3. Write two conclusions that can be made from your histogram.

_____

_____

Boston Marathon 2005
Women Finishers Under Three Hours

Place	Name (Last, First)	Official Time hh:mm:ss
1	Ndereba, Catherine	2:25:13
2	Alemu, Elfenesh	2:27:03
3	Genovese, Bruna	2:29:51
4	Zakharova, Svetlana	2:31:34
5	Biktagirova, Madina	2:32:41
6	Morgunova, Lyubov	2:33:24
7	Gemechu, Shitaye	2:33:51
8	El Kamch, Zhor	2:36:54
9	Ogawa, Mina	2:37:34
10	Olaru, Nuta	2:37:37
11	Sultanova-Zhdanova, Firaya	2:41:05
12	Levan, Emily R.	2:43:14
13	Annis, Caroline E.	2:43:46
14	Graytock, Carly E.	2:44:02
15	Sato, Yuko	2:47:00
16	Brough-Glockenmeier, Christine A.	2:49:45
17	Fagen, Kimberly E.	2:50:07
18	Rorke, Michelle M.	2:50:10
19	Piergentili, Simonetta	2:51:35
20	DiPietro, Lee	2:53:34
21	Matsubara, Eri	2:54:21
22	Haas, Lisa M.	2:54:23
23	Fulton, Diona J.	2:55:08
24	Vasseur, Nathalie	2:55:16
25	Perkins, Edie	2:55:42
26	Kondoleon, Caroline A.	2:56:04
27	Marshall, Becki J.	2:56:27
28	Fitchen-Young, Kimberly	2:56:40
29	Phelps, Danyelle L.	2:56:46
30	Nobis-Scherer, Shannon	2:56:54
31	Shertzer, Amy E.	2:57:39
32	Yamin, Regina Y.	2:57:40
33	Evjen, Rachel E.	2:57:44
34	Thorvilson, Leah M.	2:58:00
35	Phillips, Christy L.	2:58:18
36	Voghel, Lousie	2:58:56
37	Hodge, Stephanie	2:59:02
38	Haas, Kara E.	2:59:31

At the Millions of Marbles Company red marbles are very popular. There must be 4 red marbles for every 10 marbles in a package.

1. What is the ratio of red marbles to the total number of marbles in a package?

_____

2. Complete the table to show how many red marbles should be in each package.

Number of Red Marbles					
Total Number of Marbles	10	50	100	250	500

3. Explain how to find the number of red marbles in a package of 1000 marbles.

_____

_____

4. A new employee has joined the company. She must make a table for predicting the number of blue marbles in the different sized packages. There must be 2 blue marbles for every 10 marbles in each of the different sized packages. Explain how to do this for the new employee.

_____

_____

_____

_____

_____

_____

Saxon Math Course 2

In 1897 a physics professor developed the following formula for estimating the temperature by counting cricket chirps.

$$T = C + 40$$

In the formula C stands for the number of cricket chirps in 15 seconds and T stands for the temperature in degrees Fahrenheit.

1. Use the formula to complete the function table below.

C (Number of Chirps in 15 Seconds)	T (Temperature in Degrees Fahrenheit)
20	
25	
30	
35	
40	

2. Make a line graph to show the relationship between the number of chirps in 15 seconds and the temperature in degrees Fahrenheit.

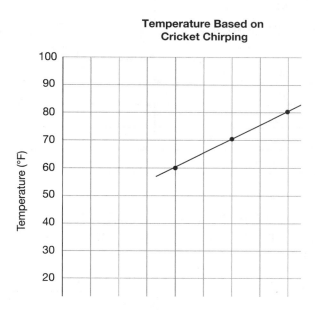

Temperature Based on Cricket Chirping

3. Use the graph to predict the temperature when there are 50 cricket chirps in 15 seconds.

_____

4. From looking at the graph, what conclusion can you draw about the relationship between cricket chirps and temperature?

_____

_____

Since 1897 formulas have been developed for various species of crickets. In the formula below for the katydid, T stands for the temperature in degrees Fahrenheit and N stands for the number of chirps in a minute.

$$\text{katydid: } T = \frac{(N + 161)}{3}$$

5. Use the formula to complete the function table below. Round your answer to the nearest degree.

N (Number of Chirps in a minute)	T (Temperature in Degrees Fahrenheit)
50	
55	
60	
65	
70	

6. a. Use the function table above to make a prediction about the temperature when a katydid chirps 75 times in one minute.

_____

b. Use the formula to find the temperature when a katydid chirps 75 times in one minute.

_____

At the Fantastic Photo Company, people can order photo albums and choose the number of sheets that hold photos. Each sheet holds 4 standard photographs. You are in charge of assembling the photo albums that the customers order.

1. Complete the table to show how many photos can be put in each album.

Number of Sheets in Album	1	2	3	4	5	6	7
Number of Photos Album Can Hold	4	8		16			

2. Write a rule to show how you can find the number of standard photos an album can hold once you know the number of sheets in an album.

_____

_____

_____

3. **a.** How many sheets are needed for 10 standard photos? Would the sheets be filled?

_____

_____

_____

b. Could an album hold filled sheets with exactly 203 photos? Why or why not?

_____

_____

Your task is help analyze data about the temperature in a room under different conditions. Use the information on **Data Sheet 13C** to answer the following questions.

1. a. Which measure of central tendency would you use to describe the average temperature in the room during Experiment A? Explain why your choice is better than another measure of central tendency for these data.

_____

_____

   b. What is the range of the temperatures in the room during experiment B?

_____

   c. The room temperature at the start of each experiment was 70°F. Find the mean temperature during Experiment C. Then find the mean temperature of the readings NOT including the start temperature. Round your calculations to the hundredths place. Explain the effect of the change in data on the mean.

_____

_____

2. a. Examine the graphs on the Data Sheet to predict which experiment is *least* likely to have the same mean and median values. Explain your reasoning.

_____

_____

   b. For the experiment you chose in Exercise 2a, predict which measure of central tendency shows a higher average temperature.

_____

   c. Using data from the table on the Data Sheet for the experiment you chose in Exercise 2a, find the mean and median temperatures. Was your prediction in Exercise 2b correct?

_____

_____

Saxon Math Course 2

3. **a.** In Experiment A, an air-conditioning unit is used to regulate the temperature in the room and the window is covered with blinds. In Experiment B, the blinds are open allowing sunlight to enter the room. Describe a possible condition that would explain the temperature readings in Experiment C. How might a change in the condition(s) you described effect the mean temperature during Experiment C?

_____

_____

_____

b. In Experiment B, the window in the room faces east. Describe how the data might be different, and how it might affect the room temperature, if the window faced south.

_____

_____

c. Which experiment produced the greatest range of temperatures? Given the conditions in Exercise 3a, explain why your answer makes sense.

_____

_____

4. **a.** Identify two ways to determine the median of the temperature readings in these experiments. Give an example of each.

_____

_____

_____

b. Comparing data from all three experiments, which Reading Time produced the greatest range of temperatures? What was the range of temperatures at that hour?

_____

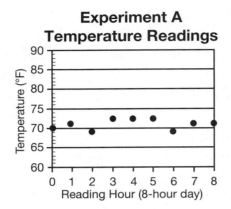

Experiment A Temperature Readings

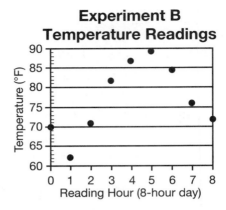

Experiment B Temperature Readings

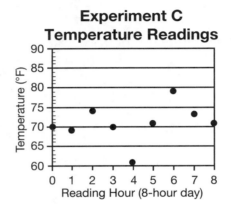

Experiment C Temperature Readings

Temperature (°F) Readings on the Hour

	0	1	2	3	4	5	6	7	8
Experiment A	70	71	69	72	72	72	69	71	71
Experiment B	70	62	71	82	87	89	84	76	72
Experiment C	70	69	74	70	61	71	79	73	71

1. Find four circular objects with different diameters that are less than 7 inches. Complete the table below to show the diameter and circumference of each. (Use a tape or string to measure the circumference or roll the object along a ruler.)

Diameter	Circumference

2. Plot the points from Excercise 1 on the grid below.

3. Draw the line of fit through the points on the graph. Use the graph to describe the relationship between the diameter and the circumference of any circle?

_____

_____

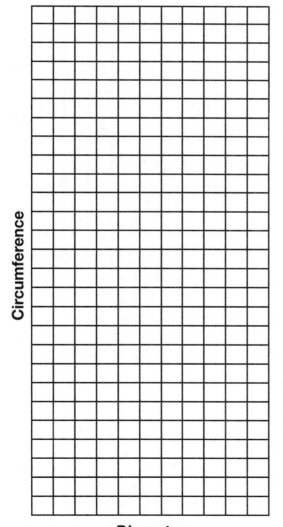

Circumference

Diameter

The President of the Perfect Paint Company has decided to honor ancient architecture while displaying the new paint colors the company created. Many structures from cultures of the past are step pyramids. The company's new colors, a metallic red, blue, and yellow, will be displayed on a step pyramid that will be used in advertising.

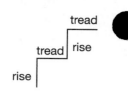

The pyramid will have 3 steps. Each step will have a rise of 1 foot and a tread of 1 foot.

The color pattern will be:

Rise	Tread	Rise	Tread	Rise	Tread
Red	Blue	Yellow	Red	Blue	Yellow

1. Draw a view of one of the sides and a view from the top on the grids below. Show the color of each section on your drawing using R for red, B for Blue, and Y for yellow.

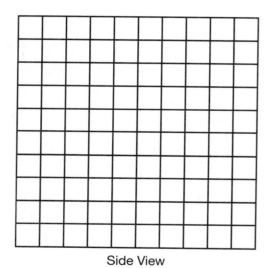

Side View

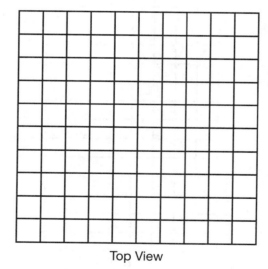

Top View

Answer these questions about the pyramid you drew in Exercise 1.

2. Find the surface area you will need to cover with each color of paint. Explain how you found your answer.

_____

_____

_____

Saxon Math Course 2

3. The table below shows the cost of each color of paint.

Paint Color	Cost Per Square Foot
Metallic Red	$0.35 per square foot
Metallic Blue	$0.20 per square foot
Metallic Yellow	$0.15 per square foot

Find the total cost of the paint it will take to cover the pyramid.

_____

_____

4. a. Design your own step pyramid display. Draw a view of one of the sides and a view from the top on the grid below. Show how you will color each section using the new colors from The Perfect Paint Company.

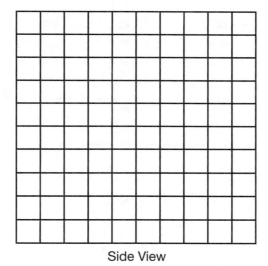

Side View   Top View

b. How much will it cost to paint your step pyramid?_____

Insert parentheses in the following equations to make them true.

1. 6 ÷ −4 + 1 = −2

2. −2 − 12 ÷ 4 = −5

_____

_____

3. −3 + 5 × −2 = −13

4. −4 + 10 ÷ −2 = −9

_____

_____

5. −4 × −5 + 3 × −6 = 2

6. 4 + 8 ÷ 1 − −2 = 4

_____

_____

Write an equation to solve each problem. Explain if you need to use order of operations to solve it.

7. The 40 people at the lake are water skiing, swimming, or on the beach. Twelve people are swimming and nine are water skiing. How many people are on the beach?

_____

_____

8. In Mr. Freeman's store, there are 7 hats displayed on each of 3 shelves. Mr. Freeman sold 5 hats. How many hats have not been sold?

_____

_____

9. Write your own word problem. Make sure you need to use the order of operations to solve it.

_____

_____

As an employee for Main Street Hardware Store, your task is to set up discounts for a sale on four items. You need to set up a plan for the sale where each item is marked with a different discount.

30% off the regular price

$\frac{1}{4}$ off

10% off

$\frac{1}{3}$ off

The sale will last until all of the items are gone. Your goal is to generate sales totaling at least $1500 once all the items have been sold.

1. Complete the table below to show the discount that you will give to each item and the new price of each item.

Item	Regular Price	Amount in Stock	Discount	New Price
Nails	$2 per pound	100 pounds		
Fencing	$3 per foot	400 feet		
Hammers	$12 apiece	20		
Lawn Mowers	$75	8		

2. Explain how your plan will bring in at least $1500 from the sale when all the items are sold.

_____

_____

_____

_____

_____

_____

Answer these questions using the data in Exercise 1.

3. Write an equation to show the amount of money the store will receive from the sale of any amount of nails.

_____

4. **a.** Write a ratio that shows the amount of money you expect to make from the sale of the hammers to the amount of money you expect to make in all.

_____

b. Suppose everything is sold except for half of the hammers. How would the ratio from 4a change? Can you just take half of each number in the ratio from 4a and make a new ratio. Why or why not?

_____

_____

_____

_____

_____

5. Suppose you want to put a saw that regularly sells for $40 on sale for 20% off and a drill that regularly sells for $90 on sale for 10% off.

Will you be taking more money off the price of the saw than the price of the drill since 20% is more than 10%. Why or why not?

_____

_____

_____

_____

Name _____

State if you would use mental math, estimation, paper and pencil, or a calculator to solve each problem below. You must use each method once. For each problem, explain why you made your choice.

1. The school needs 300 boxes of pencils. The pencils cost $5 a box. You want to find out how much the pencils will cost.

   _____

   _____

2. You are at the grocery store. You have the following items in your cart:

   carton of milk ....$1.35   oranges $3.25
   squash..........................$0.93   can of tomatoes $2.17
   chicken.........................$4.12   onions.......................$1.89
   paper towels.................$5.79   apple juice $3.98

   You want to find out about how much the total will be before you get to the checkout counter.

   _____

   _____

3. You are balancing your checkbook. Since you found that the balance in your checking account was $326.42, you have written checks for the following amounts:

   $93.68, $10.65, $9.54, $6.97

   You want to find out exactly how much money is left in your account.

   _____

   _____

4. You are at the store and you buy two items for $15.98 and $29.56. You want to know what the exact total is so you can give the exact amount to the clerk.

   _____

   _____

Name _____

Suppose you perform a probability experiment in which you roll two number cubes one at a time, and record the outcome as a two-digit number. For example, if you roll 3 and then a 2, the outcome is 32. Answer the questions about this probability experiment.

1. In a table or a tree diagram show all of the possible two-digit numbers that could be an outcome of this experiment. Explain how you organized your answer to make sure that you had all of the possible outcomes.

_____

_____

_____

_____

2. What is the probability of an outcome being a prime number in this experiment? Explain how you got your answer.

_____

_____

_____

_____

Saxon Math Course 2

Answer these questions about the probability experiment in Exercise 1.

3. What is the probability of the outcome being a composite number when you toss two number cubes? Explain how you got your answer.

_____

_____

_____

4. What is the probability of the outcome being a prime or a composite number? Explain how you got your answer.

_____

_____

5. What is the probability of the outcome being a number that is a factor of itself? Explain how you got your answer.

_____

_____

6. What is the probability of the outcome being a number that is a factor of 10? Explain how you got your answer.

_____

_____

7. What is the probability of the outcome being a number that is a factor of 100? Explain how you got your answer.

_____

_____

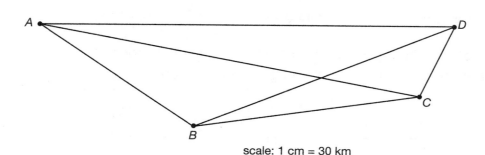

Distances
A to D = 11 cm
A to B = 5 cm
B to C = 6 cm
D to C = 2 cm
A to C = 10.5 cm

scale: 1 cm = 30 km

1. Write an equation to show how many kilometers a distance on the map actually is. Explain why your equation works.

_____

_____

_____

2. What is the difference between the distance from Town A to Town B and from Town A to Town C? Write an equation and give the answer.

_____

3. Mr. Wong traveled from Town A to Town D and then to Town C. How many kilometers did he travel in all? Write an equation and give the answer.

_____

4. Formulate a problem about the map that goes with the equation
$y = 330 - 180$.

_____

_____

_____

5. Formulate a problem about the map. Write an equation to solve the problem. Solve the equation.

_____

_____

_____

Saxon Math Course 2

You have been hired to draw conclusions from the 2000 United States census for a Web site about the United States. Use the graph of the population in the United States from 1960 to 2000 for the exercises below.

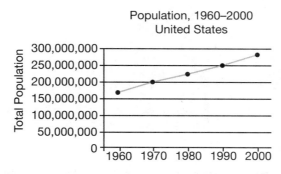

Population, 1960–2000
United States

1. Make a convincing argument to support the following inference made from the data in the graph.

The population in the United States in 1995 was about 265,000,000.

_____

_____

_____

_____

2. Make an inference from the graph and a convincing argument to support it.

_____

_____

_____

_____

Use the graph of the age distribution in the United States in 2000 for the exercises below.

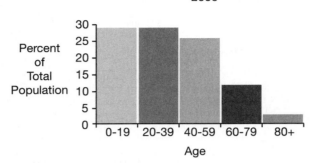

Population Age Distribution
2000

3. Make a convincing argument to support the following inference made from the data in the graph.

   In the year 2000, about 55% of the population was 20 to 59 years of age.

   _____

   _____

   _____

   _____

4. Make an inference from the graph and a convincing argument to support it.

   _____

   _____

   _____

   _____

 Saxon Math Course 2

Your job is to help the Director of the Architecture Museum with models. Today you will make two regular square pyramid models.

1. Each of the triangular faces on Pyramid *A* has sides that measure 5 centimeters, 5 centimeters, and 6 centimeters. Are all four of these triangular faces similar? Are all four of these triangular faces congruent? Explain your thinking.

   _____

   _____

2. Each of the triangular faces on Pyramid *B* has sides that measure 7.5 centimeters, 7.5 centimeters, and 9 centimeters. Are the triangular faces on Pyramid *B* similar to the triangular faces on Pyramid *A*? Show how you reached your conclusion.

   _____

   _____

3. Make models of the two pyramids using Activity Sheets 22B and C. Does it look like the two pyramids are similar? Why do you think the pyramids are similar or not similar?

   _____

   _____

   _____

   _____

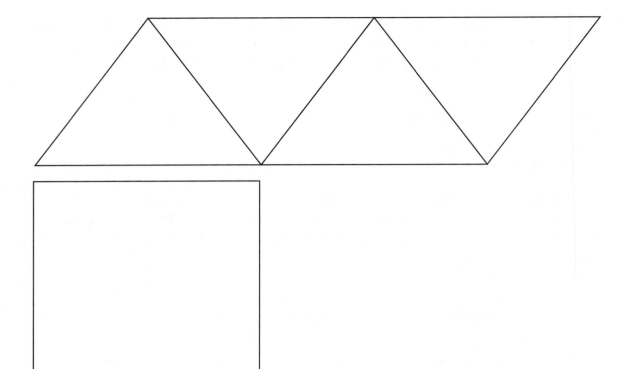

Saxon Math Course 2

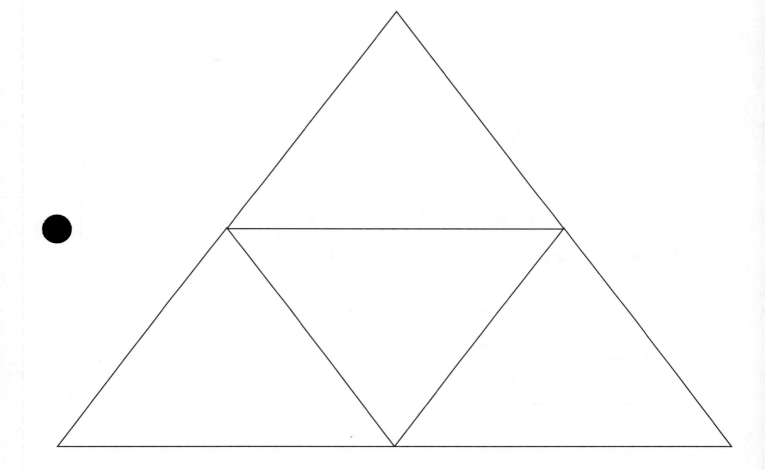

Name _____

As an employee of The Wood Toy and Puzzle Company, you are responsible for the packaging of wood puzzles. You must solve problems you encounter as you design the packaging.

1. The wood puzzles are packaged in cube-shaped boxes.

   a. Make a net of a cube with a surface area of 24 sq. in.

   b. What is the length of each edge of the cube? _____

2. What is the volume of the cube? Explain how you got your answer.

_____

_____

_____

_____

_____

_____

       Saxon Math Course 2

Answer questions 3–5. Use the cubic box from Exercise 1.

3. The company wants to make pyramids, cylinders, spheres, and cones that are as large as possible and will still fit in the cube-shaped box. Complete the table to give the dimensions and volume of each of the figures.

Figure	Dimensions	Volume
pyramid		
cylinder		
sphere		
cone		

4. How did you find the volume of the cone?

_____

_____

_____

5. If the company decides to make a cubic box where the edges are double that of the box in Excercise 1, how does the volume of the box change? Explain your answer.

_____

_____

_____

_____

Finding Missing Numbers in Equations

Equation	Operation
$4 + n = 7$	To find a missing addend, we subtract. $4 + n = 7$
$n + 5 = 9$	To find a missing addend, we subtract. $n + 5 = 9$
$n - 2 = 7$	To find a missing minuend, we add. $n - 2 = 7$
$6 - n = 1$	To find a missing subtrahend, we subtract. $6 - n = 1$
$6n = 12$	To find a missing factor, we divide. $6n = 12$
$n \times 7 = 14$	To find a missing factor, we divide. $n \times 7 = 14$
$\dfrac{6}{n} = 2$	To find a missing divisor, we divide. $\dfrac{6}{n} = 2$
$\dfrac{n}{4} = 8$	To find a missing dividend, we multiply. $\dfrac{n}{4} = 8$

Checks

My Street _____

My Town, USA _____

Date _____

Pay to the
order of ____ *Modern Homes* _____ $ _*1,536,000*_

One million, five hundred thirty-six thousand _____ DOLLARS

THIS CHECK IS NONNEGOTIABLE, FOR EDUCATION PURPOSES ONLY

My Street _____

My Town, USA _____

Date _____

Pay to the
order of ____ *Bicycle Shop* _____ $ _*36.85*_

_____ DOLLARS

THIS CHECK IS NONNEGOTIABLE, FOR EDUCATION PURPOSES ONLY

_____

_____

_____

Date _____

Pay to the
order of _____ $ _____

_____ DOLLARS

THIS CHECK IS NONNEGOTIABLE, FOR EDUCATION PURPOSES ONLY

_____

_____

_____

Date _____

Pay to the
order of _____ $ _____

_____ DOLLARS

THIS CHECK IS NONNEGOTIABLE, FOR EDUCATION PURPOSES ONLY

Saxon Math Course 2

Divisibility

Number	Divisible by 2	Divisible by 3	Divisible by 4	Divisible by 5	Divisible by 6	Divisible by 8	Divisible by 9	Divisible by 10

Halves

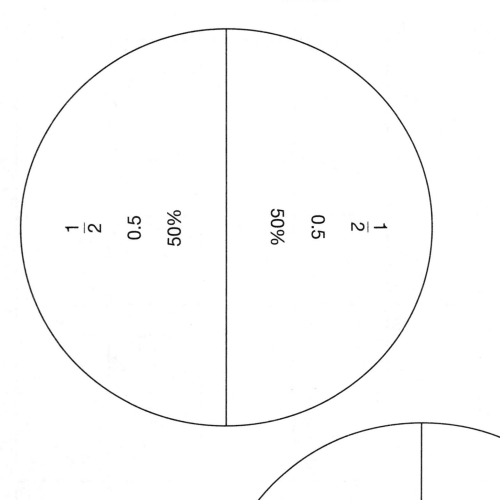

$\frac{1}{2}$
0.5
50%

50%
0.5
$\frac{1}{2}$

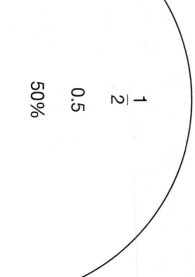

$\frac{1}{2}$
0.5
50%

50%
0.5
$\frac{1}{2}$

Thirds

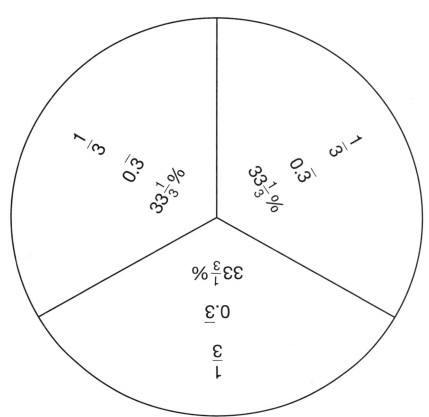

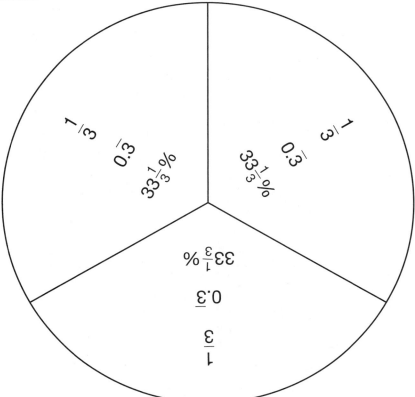

Fourths

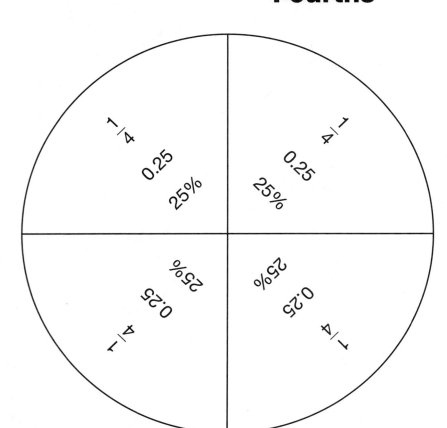

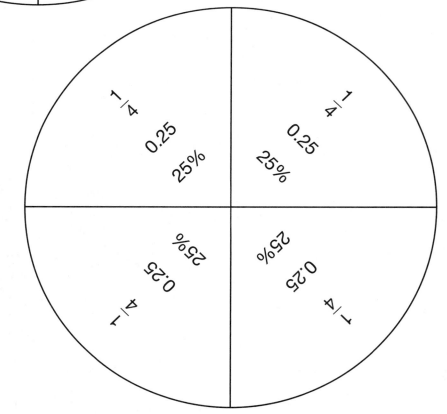

Sixths

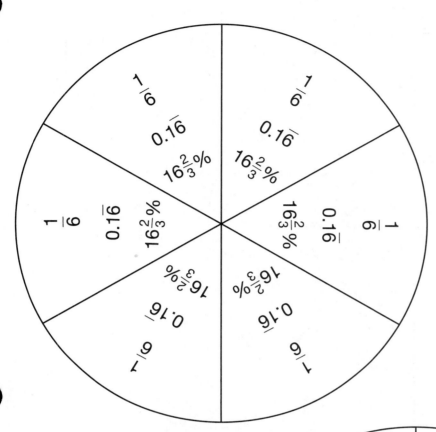

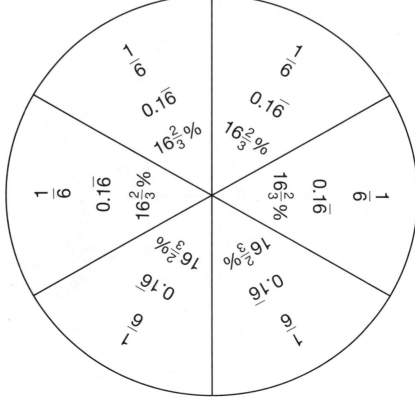

Eighths

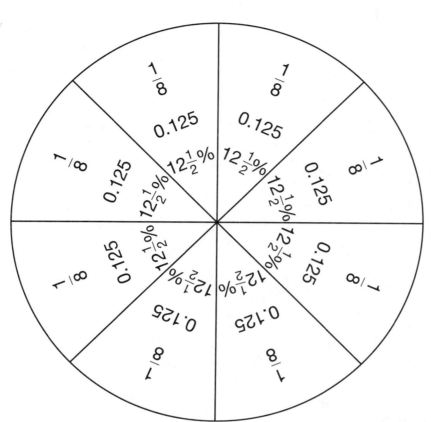

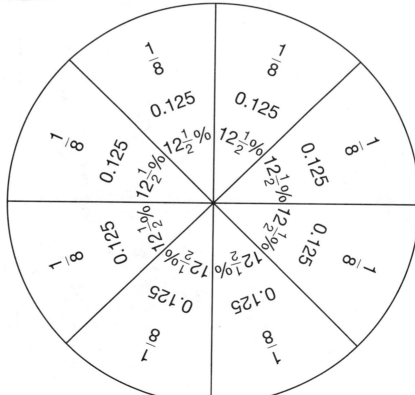

Saxon Math Course 2

Twelfths

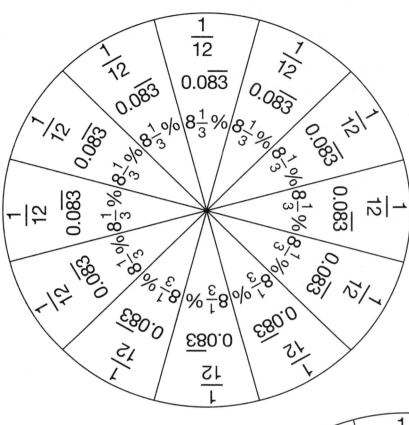

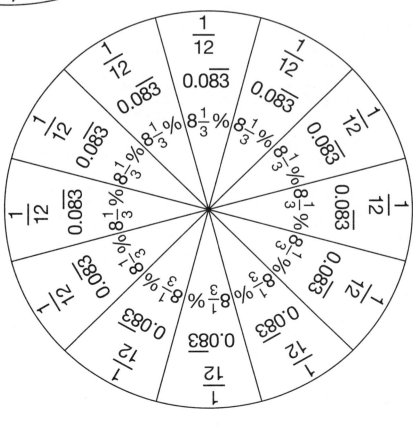

Measuring Angles

Use a protractor to find the following angle measures:

1. m∠AOB _____

2. m∠AOC _____

3. m∠EOD _____

4. m∠AOD _____

5. m∠EOB _____

6. m∠BOG _____

7. m∠EOF _____

8. m∠EOG _____

9. m∠AOF _____

10. m∠EOA _____

11. m∠DOB _____

12. m∠COF _____

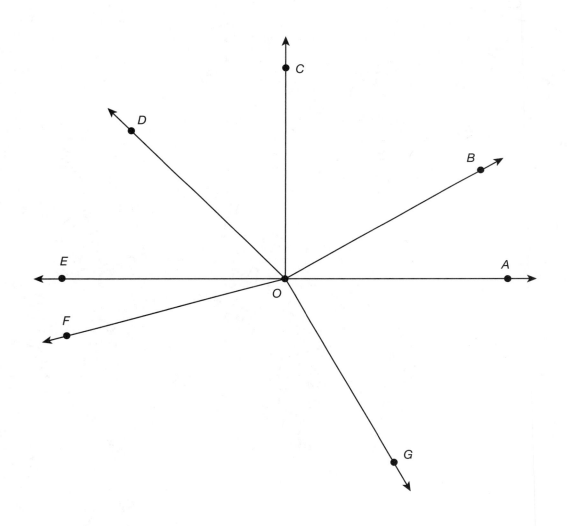

Saxon Math Course 2

Hundred Number Chart

1	2	3	4	5	6	7	8	9	10
11	12	13	14	15	16	17	18	19	20
21	22	23	24	25	26	27	28	29	30
31	32	33	34	35	36	37	38	39	40
41	42	43	44	45	46	47	48	49	50
51	52	53	54	55	56	57	58	59	60
61	62	63	64	65	66	67	68	69	70
71	72	73	74	75	76	77	78	79	80
81	82	83	84	85	86	87	88	89	90
91	92	93	94	95	96	97	98	99	100

Sample Menu

Soups and Salads

Salads are served with a choice of dressing and an assorted breadbasket.

Chicken Salad or Tuna Salad $5.75

  Served on a bed of romaine lettuce and garnished with tomato, onions, and hardboiled egg.

Tossed Salad $2.95

Soup of the Day   Cup...........................$2.39
                         Bowl $3.80

Sandwiches

1/4 lb. Hamburger $2.75

              with cheese, add $0.35

Grilled Cheese...$2.25

Hot Dog $1.75

Grilled Chicken $2.79

Side Orders

French Fries..$0.99

Potato Salad...$1.35

Baked Potato...$1.35

Coleslaw..$0.95

Green Beans..$0.95

Beverages

Orange Juice $1.15

Coffee...$0.75

Milk..$1.25

Tea...$0.75

Hot Cocoa $1.45

Soda $1.29

Bottled Water $1.35

Coordinate Plane

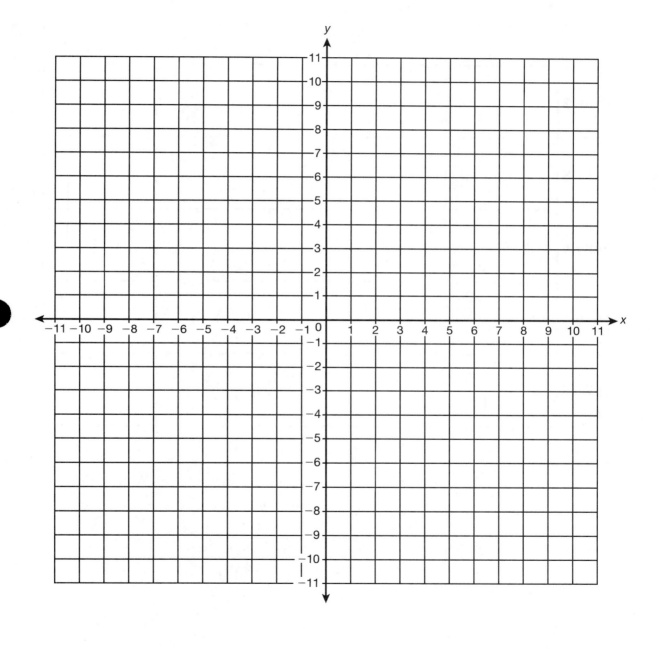

Exponential Patterns

	Column 1	Column 2	Column 3	Column 4
Row 1	$\dfrac{10^6}{10^3}$	$\dfrac{10 \cdot 10 \cdot 10 \cdot 10 \cdot 10 \cdot 10}{10 \cdot 10 \cdot 10}$	10^3	1000
Row 2	$\dfrac{10^5}{10^3}$			
Row 3	$\dfrac{10^4}{10^3}$			
Row 4				
Row 5				
Row 6				

Saxon Math Course 2

Number Lines

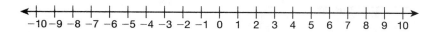

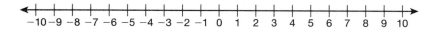

Quadrilaterals

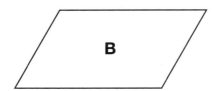

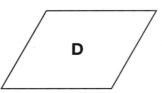

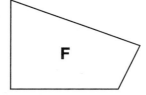

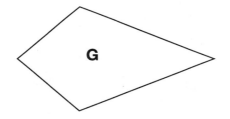

Angle–Side Relationships in Triangles

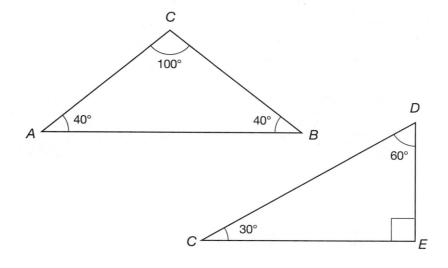

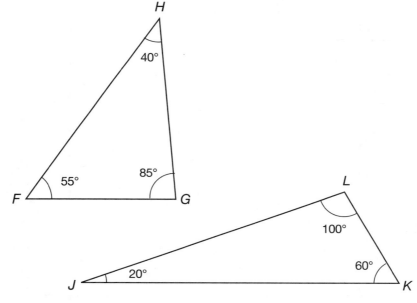

Estimating Pi

Measure and record the diameter and circumference of two or three circular objects. For each object measured, divide the circumference by the diameter and record the answer, rounded to two decimal places, in the fourth column. Record the results from other student groups to extend the list.

Object	Circumference	Diameter	Circumference Diameter

Saxon Math Course 2

Transformations

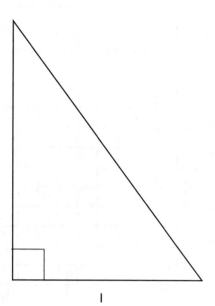

I

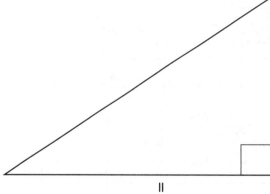

II

Probability Experiment

Section A: Possible outcomes of rolling a pair of dice

Outcome of First Die

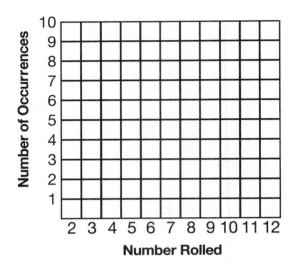

	2	3	4	5	6	7
	3	4	5	6	7	8
	4	5	6	7	8	9
	5	6	7	8	9	10
	6	7	8	9	10	11
	7	8	9	10	11	12

Outcome of Second Die

Section B: Theoretical outcomes of 36 rolls of a pair of dice

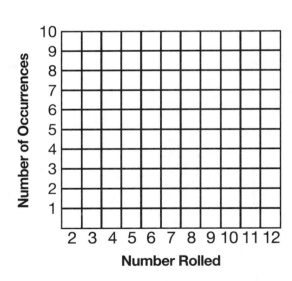

Section C: Actual results of rolling a pair of dice 36 times

Number Rolled	Tally
2	
3	
4	
5	
6	
7	
8	
9	
10	
11	
12	

Section D: Possible reasons for a difference between theoretical outcome and actual results

Saxon Math Course 2

Polygons

Regular Polygon	Number of sides	Number of triangles formed	Sum of interior angles	Measure of each interior angle
△				
▢				
⬠				
⬡				
(heptagon)				
(octagon)				
Pattern	n			

Clocks

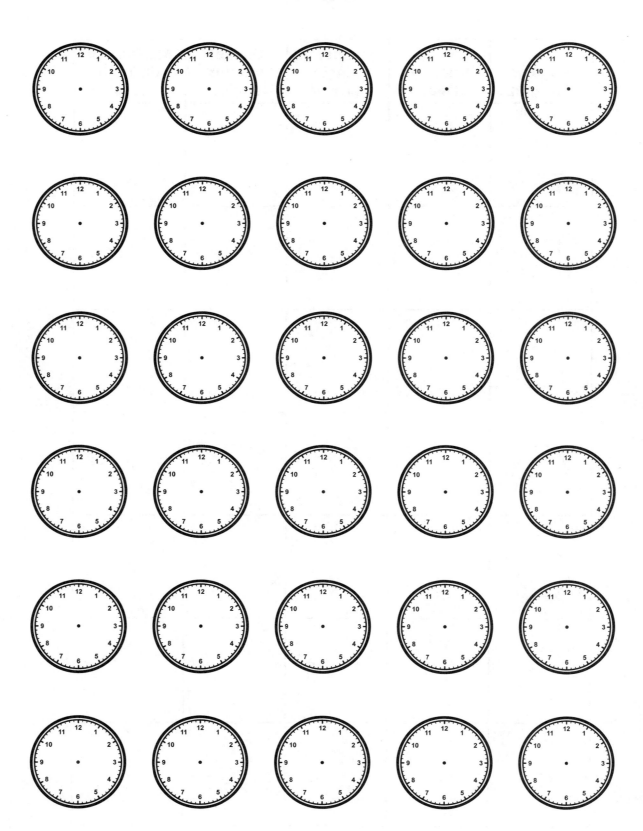

Saxon Math Course 2

Slope

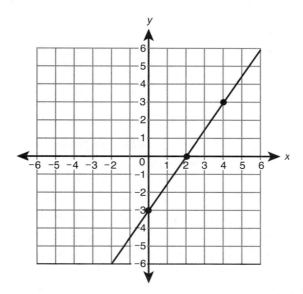

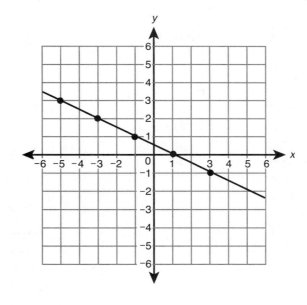

Slope

Calculate the slope of each line *a–h* below.

1. Slope of line *a:* _____

2. Slope of line *b:* _____

3. Slope of line *c:* _____

4. Slope of line *d:* _____

5. Slope of line *e:* _____

6. Slope of line *f:* _____

7. Slope of line *g:* _____

8. Slope of line *h:* _____

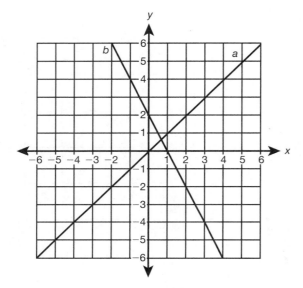

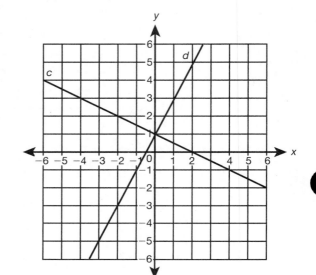

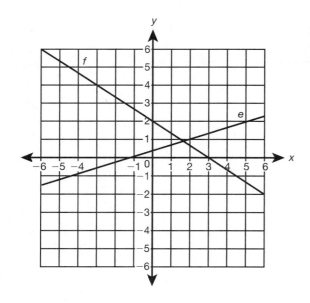

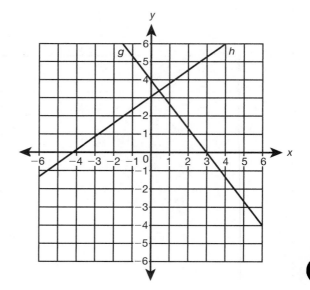

Saxon Math Course 2

Square Centimeter Grid

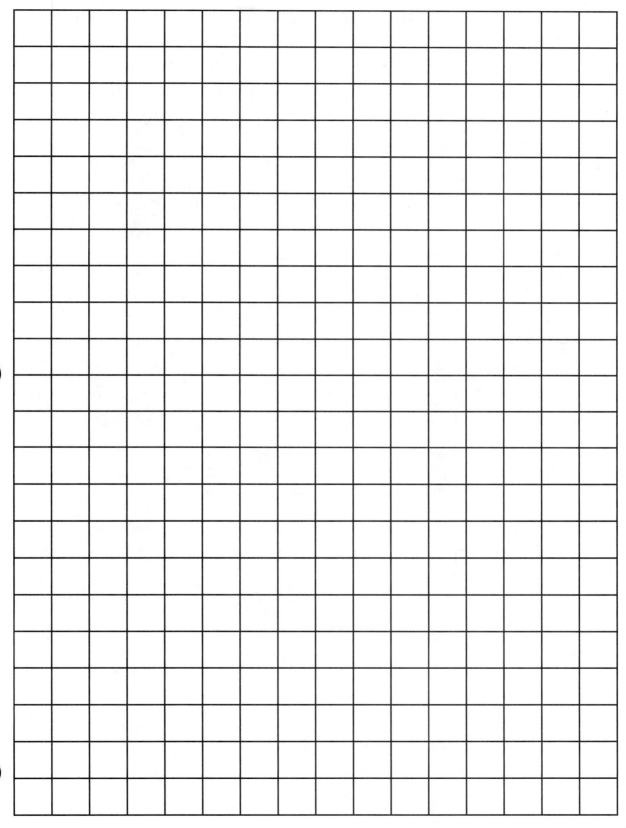

Tetrahedron and Cube Patterns

Tetrahedron (four-faced polyhedron)

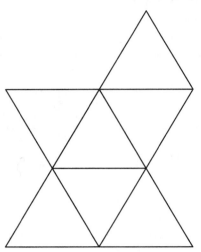

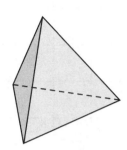

Cube

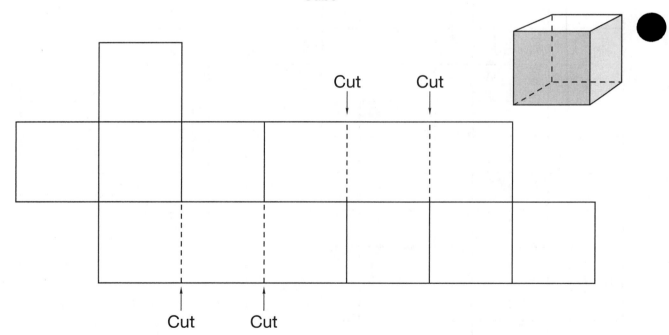

Cut   Cut

Cut   Cut

Saxon Math Course 2

Octahedron and Dodecahedron Patterns

Octahedron

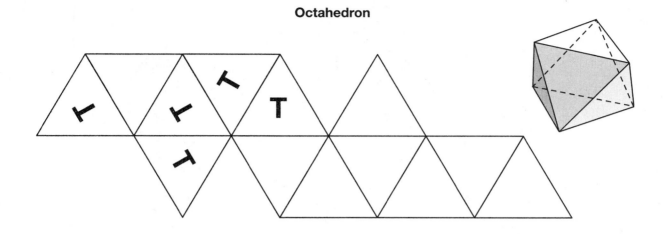

Dodecahedron

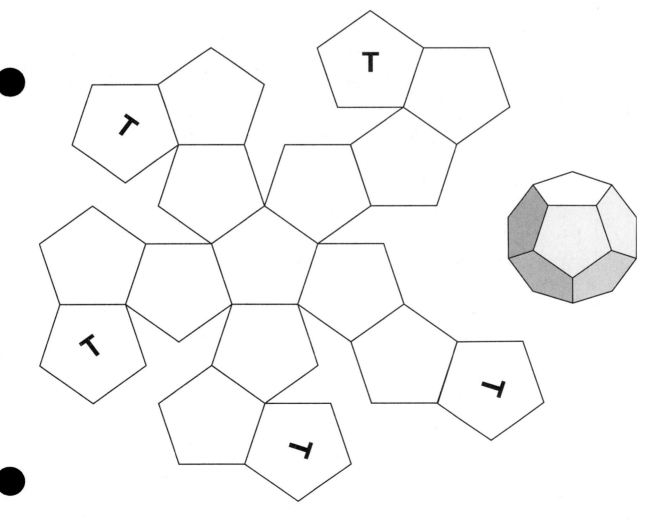

Icosahedron Pattern

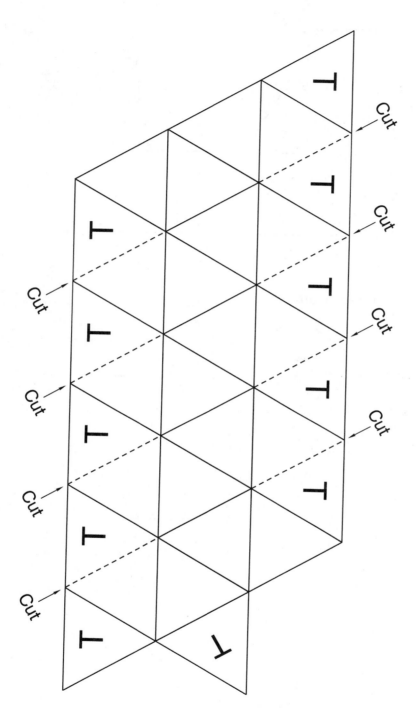

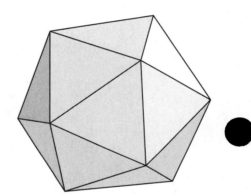

Saxon Math Course 2